Alone
Together

ALONE TOGETHER

by Lawrence Roman

Nelson Doubleday, Inc.
Garden City, New York

To Evelyn

AUTHOR'S NOTE ON PRODUCTION

While the Broadway stage accommodated a full two-story house, the play loses none of its effectiveness if the Butler house is split-level, thereby eliminating the need for a high stage.

An effective set would be a Spanish-style split-level, reflecting Helene's taste, with just a few steps leading up to a balcony off which the bedrooms are. Brown beams, arched windows, and stucco walls would make for a warm, homey environment on which to play.

Another point which may prove to be a small problem is "traveling" Keith's car north from Los Angeles to Seattle on the map of the United States in the first scene. This can be solved in two ways. If the map is small, for a smaller house, a magnet behind the map can be manipulated unseen by George, enabling him to "travel" the metal button which stands for Keith's car. On Broadway, where a large map was used, a track was built into which Keith's "car" fit, enabling George to do the same thing.

ALONE TOGETHER was originally presented at The Whole Theatre Company and subsequently opened in New York at the Music Box Theatre on October 21, 1984, with the following cast:

GEORGE BUTLER	*Kevin McCarthy*
HELENE BUTLER	*Janis Paige*
KEITH BUTLER	*Dennis Drake*
MICHAEL BUTLER	*Don Howard*
ELLIOTT BUTLER	*Kevin O'Rourke*
JANIE JOHNSON	*Alexandra Gersten*

Produced by Arnold Mittelman and Lynne Peyser
Directed by Arnold Mittelman
Scenery by Karl Eigsti
Costumes by Jane Greenwood
Lighting by Arden Fingerhut
Production Stage Manager, Larry Forde

Alone
Together

CAST
(in order of appearance)

GEORGE BUTLER, 53
HELENE BUTLER, 50
KEITH BUTLER, 19
MICHAEL BUTLER, 30
ELLIOTT BUTLER, 28
JANIE JOHNSON, 18

The action takes place in the Butler home in Los Angeles. The time is the present.

ACT ONE

ACT TWO

ACT ONE

ACT ONE

Scene 1

The Butler home in Los Angeles, on the West Side, within minutes of the Pacific Ocean. Two stories, or split-level. A balcony leads to three doors which are the bedrooms of the three sons the Butlers have raised. Downstairs: living room, dining room, kitchen. The parents' bedroom cannot be seen, nor can the swimming pool and hot tub in the yard. This is the house in which Helene and George Butler raised Michael (now 30), Elliott (now 28), and Keith (now 19). Solidly middle class, the Butlers are a traditional family.

The time is the present. September. Morning.

At rise: Keith, preparing to leave for college, is in his bedroom getting his things together. George is downstairs putting some of Keith's things by the door. Helene is in kitchen stuffing a shopping bag with pre-wrapped sandwiches. She calls upstairs.

HELENE: Keith! Don't forget to put the barbells away! I don't want Dad dragging them!

KEITH: *(Appearing on balcony)* Will do, Mom!

HELENE: And the surfboards! Put them in the garage with the scuba stuff! And, please, take down those horrid posters of yours!

KEITH: Already did!

(Goes back into his room. As will become apparent, Helene is in a pivotal time in her life. Betwixt and between, as it were, so ambivalence prevails. A number of feelings are going on within her simultaneously, so her mood shifts rapidly)

GEORGE: How do you feel?

HELENE: *(That ambivalence)* Both ways. Sad he's going, glad he's going. I'm just about breaking even. *(Goes back to her work in kitchen)*

GEORGE: I'm 60-40. On the glad side. Hard to believe, isn't it? Keith's off to college. The last of them. First time in 30 years we're going to be totally our own people.

(Keith comes bounding down with some of his things)

KEITH: Dad, catch. *(Throws George football . . . About the things he carries:)* You got room for this?

GEORGE: Tennis racket, golf clubs, backpack. I can see you're going to get a lot of studying done.

KEITH: Creative loafing, Dad. *(Gives George two books)* Return these to the library for me, will you, please?

GEORGE: When are they due?

KEITH: Don't ask. Just put them in the drop and run like hell.

GEORGE: Yeah, that's what I thought.

(Keith takes a sweater from sofa. George takes it from him)

GEORGE: Mine! *(They start out with some of Keith's things)* Check the tires?

KEITH: They're okay.

GEORGE: Windshield wipers? You can run into rain up there.

KEITH: No problem, Dad. I'm grown up. I know all about rain.

(They are out as phone rings)

HELENE: Hello! . . . Oh, hi, Martha. *(Works as she talks)* Yes, Keith's about ready to go now . . . Me? Lord, I've waited so long for this moment, it's like coming out of a tunnel! . . . Sorry, can't make lunch. George is treating me to a full day at Elizabeth Arden. The works! . . . Yes, I know that's unusual for me, but I plan to make the most of it . . . Sorry, dinner's out too. *(Sexual innuendo)* George and I have plans of our own. *(Small smile. Keith returns)* Got to go! Talk to you later. *(Hangs up)* Here, dear. *(She slips Keith cash with a "shh," meaning don't tell Dad, then gives him stuffed shopping bag)*

KEITH: What's in it?

HELENE: Chicken sandwiches.

KEITH: *(Hefts bag)* Great! Should carry me through the end of the semester.

HELENE: There's something else in it.

(George enters as Keith takes a long, knit red scarf, which seems to be endless, out of the bag)

KEITH: Hey, that's great, Mom! You made it, huh? *(Whips scarf around his neck)* The Red Baron strikes again! Sure hope those women up there are ready for these California good looks.

GEORGE: They radioed down they're gathering at the state line.

(Laughter. The moment to say good-bye)

KEITH: Well, I guess this is it. 'Bye, Dad. *(They shake hands)*

GEORGE: 'Bye, son. Now look, if you run into any problems . . .

(Hiding it from Helene, George slips Keith some cash as Helene did. Keith pockets it happily)

KEITH: Dad, I'm 19, for God's sake. Something happens, I'll handle it myself . . . 'Bye, Mom.

(She fusses with his hair, strokes his face motherly as:)

KEITH: Don't forget, I'm staying with Dave in San Francisco for a while. I'll phone down as soon as I get settled in Seattle. I'll call Mike and Elliott too.

HELENE: 'Bye, dear.

(They embrace. George picks up a movie camera. Photographs his son about to leave the nest)

HELENE: I love you.

KEITH: Me too, Mom. *(Keith grimaces as he realizes father is photographing him)* Well, it's been real. *(Starting out)* Now don't worry. I promise I'll drive carefully, study hard, and mail home my dirty clothes.

HELENE: Don't you dare! *(She sees sweater that George had taken away from Keith)* You forgot this.

GEORGE: Hey, that's mine.

(Helene has taken the sweater out to Keith. George also exits the front door, still photographing his departing son. Now we realize someone is around the side of the house. From outside, a cloth bag is thrown in. It clanks as though it contains metal. Now a duffel bag comes flying in. Now a scruffy-looking figure, hair wild, clothing Army surplus, climbs in. He is Michael (30), the Butlers' oldest son. Though young, Michael is the prototypical absentminded professor. Moreover, he doesn't mind letting his parents know how deeply he can suffer. He picks up his things, looks out front of house where his parents and brother are loading the car, then goes upstairs to his bedroom. Meanwhile, ad libs as Keith says "see you at Christmas" . . . good-byes . . . Keith's car pulls away. Pause. Helene and George come back into their "empty nest")

GEORGE: Bastille Day!

(Helene laughs)

I've got a present for you.

HELENE: Whatever it is, I deserve it.

(George gets a map of the United States)

Just what I've always wanted. A map of the United States.

GEORGE: Not just a map. A situation map. I'll show you.
*(He places the map on a high place in good audience
view, produces little buttons)* Michael. At MIT. *(He affixes button on Boston)* Elliott. With Nancy in Dallas.
(He affixes button on Dallas) Keith. *(Using magnet behind map, He travels Keith's "car" up the West Coast as
Keith would be driving, and screeches to a halt in Seattle)*

HELENE: George, you've done it again. What a marvelous
idea!

GEORGE: You and me . . . Face it, honey, they're gone.
All of them. We have raised three great sons and passed
them on to the world. The crisis clinic is closed.

HELENE: And I'm ready. You have no idea. It's even hard
to remember life before motherhood. It seems I went
straight from hula-hooping into gestation.

(George laughs. These are two people who like each other)

Is it really true, is it? Order? Freedom? Privacy? Honestly,
I think that's the hardest part with kids around, never
being alone. I'm tempted to cover all the mirrors and
drift about naked.

(George turns and starts to leave)

George, I didn't mean to scare you off already . . . Where are you going?

GEORGE: To rip out Keith's pot plants.

(Helene turns on tape deck)

HELENE: Do it later. *(A song is heard)* Our music. Softly. Thirty seconds of that and my hearing's improved already. *(They dance)* Then it's true. I *am* sprung. I can do anything I want, even nothing.

GEORGE: All you have to do is learn how.

HELENE: Maybe now *I* can get sick.

GEORGE: Helene, it's our time and right on schedule. Money's okay, if we don't go crazy. I've got the time. I've got some good young accountants to handle the office. The page has been turned. We're down to birthday and holiday visits.

HELENE: *(They stop dancing)* We did a good job with them, didn't we?

GEORGE: On a scale of ten, eight.

HELENE: Elliott may be an eight. I'm afraid Michael may only be a seven.

GEORGE: How can you say that? He's a genius.

HELENE: At math. At other things I'm not so sure. Remember what Dr. Friedman said: He's grown up very uneven.

GEORGE: Well, Keith's a nine, so the average holds.

(Helene smiles, reassured)

HELENE: Yeah, for an accident he may have turned out to be the solidest.

GEORGE: Two to practice on, one to get just right.

HELENE: *(Very up, pulls away from him)* Oh, I'm so excited, I don't know what to do first! . . . George, I hope you won't be disappointed, but I don't plan on anything big right off. I think I'll just go in for petty gratification. And I don't plan on spending time finding myself. I haven't been lost, just under siege . . . Maybe UCLA has a class in frivolity. After raising three boys how I can get behind being useless.

GEORGE: Not you. I don't believe it. You've got something up your sleeve.

HELENE: *(Evasively)* Maybe . . . What do you see?

GEORGE: An open bedroom door. Love whenever. Trips at the spur of the moment, just the two of us. *(He produces travel folders)* Let's go to Bora Bora. I've always wanted to see the South Seas.

(Already they are on different wavelengths)

HELENE: *(Doesn't care for that)* Bora Bora! George, really. I don't have much interest in native women stripped to the waist. Let's go to Europe.

GEORGE: Helene, we've been to Europe.

HELENE: With the kids when they were little. Tivoli Gardens got a full day, the Louvre got a brisk walk-through . . . I want to see the Prado in Madrid, the Hermitage in Leningrad . . .

GEORGE: Russia? My God, they say the food's awful.

HELENE: We'll brown-bag it. Now don't start bending things your way again . . .

GEORGE: My way? What do you mean my way? We always talk things out . . .

HELENE: George, I don't want to start arguing right off.

GEORGE: We're not arguing. We don't argue, we discuss.

HELENE: George, you and I. One on one. Except for occasional vacations we haven't been alone since the Fifties. *(It worries her)* Does it worry you?

GEORGE: Nope.

HELENE: No kids as buffer in between. No skirting our problems because they've dumped one on us we could hide behind.

GEORGE: What problems? We get along beautifully.

HELENE: *(Cuddling)* Yes, for a husband, I guess you've worn pretty well.

GEORGE: I love you too. I can tell. I still enjoy watching you sleep.

HELENE: Thank you, dear . . . Martha called. She
wanted us to join her and Bill for dinner tonight. I told
her we had plans.

GEORGE: I bought four kinds of cheese, three kinds of
fruit, and two bottles of Montrachet.

HELENE: I've got a candle that burns different colors and a
Presto log that lasts for hours.

GEORGE: I hope you don't expect the same from me . . .
How long has it been since we made love in front of the
fireplace?

HELENE: Nine months before Michael was born.

GEORGE: *(Laughs, then:)* Remember when they were lit-
tle we'd give them breakfast, turn on the TV, then run
upstairs and make love while they watched "Howdy
Doody." We sure had to get a lot done in half an hour.
Come on, let's get started. You're due at Elizabeth
Arden's and I've got some IRS guys to meet.

(They start out of house)

HELENE: Call your mother. She'll want to know Keith got
off all right.

GEORGE: I'll call tonight. Every time I ring her down at
Leisure World I interrupt her poker game.

*(They are gone . . . Now Michael comes down, goes to
refrigerator. As he dials long distance, starting with area
code 617, he takes a tray of cheese out of the refrigerator.
Bites into the cheddar. He gets a bottle of wine out of the*

refrigerator, is impressed by the label. Gets bottle opener.
Meanwhile)

MICHAEL: Brenda. It's me . . . L.A. . . . My folks' house
. . . I left you a note . . . Why did I have to sign it?
How many guys are you living with? . . . Brenda, it has
nothing to do with you, you know that, but I thought it
through and I know how I feel. If Professor Neumann
calls, which he won't, tell him you don't know where I
am . . . Yeah, jot it down. Area code 213-434-3880 . . .
Don't worry about it, call collect . . . Yeah, okay, I miss
you.

(He hangs up. Wine bottle and cheese in tow, he starts for
stairs. Stops as he sees the map of the United States, the
situation map. For a moment he studies it, then figures it
out. He takes the "Michael" button off Boston and puts it
next to the "Helene-George" button on Los Angeles. Starts
upstairs for his bedroom)

LIGHTS OUT

Scene 2

The same. That evening. Small fire in fireplace. George, in robe, is at refrigerator, getting cheese. Helene, wrapping robe around herself, is coming in from yard.

HELENE: I'm so relaxed. Whoever invented the hot tub should run the government.

GEORGE: Honey, did you see the cheddar? I've got the brie, the stilton, the triple creme . . .

HELENE: *(Broaching serious subject)* George, I ran into Ralph Goode the other day. *(No response from George)* I had lunch with him.

GEORGE: That's funny. I thought I put both bottles of wine in here. Did you take one?

HELENE: Not me. One bottle is plenty.

GEORGE: *(Is opening wine)* Right. What were you saying about Ralph Goode.

HELENE: Ralph remembered those paintings I'd done so long ago. He said if I turned out a series of beach scenes he liked, he'd put them in his gallery! Oh, not the Beverly Hills one, the one in the valley.

GEORGE: So that's what you've got up your sleeve! I knew something was perking. I think it's great! Why were you so coy about telling me? *(Will pour and give her glass)*

HELENE: You know. I've started and stopped so many times before, I didn't want to make any grand statements. I thought I'd get going again when Michael and Elliott began to grow up. Then Keith came along. I tried when Michael and Elliott left . . . but Keith always seemed to need so much. And the house and your folks and my folks. I hope you don't mind but I'm going to turn the dressing room into a studio and paint there. *(As much to pump herself up)* I've got to get with it if I'm going to do it at all.

GEORGE: You will, you'll see, you're on your way!

(They toast and click glasses. George gestures for her to sit. He exits and returns with a white fur rug which he gleefully spreads out in front of the fireplace. Helene smiles, then:)

HELENE: You know, a lot of times I never thought we'd get this far. I think if I had had any nerve I'd have dumped you long ago.

GEORGE: Yeah. What was the hardest part?

HELENE: Getting you out of your 30s into your 40s. It was like pulling you through a keyhole! . . . You started playing around, didn't you?

GEORGE: Me?! No!

HELENE: Of course you did.

GEORGE: I did not! So help me! Never!

HELENE: You did! Look, I'm not putting down names and dates at this late stage, and I'm not saying I wasn't hurt. I was. Terribly. I'm just saying you did and I knew you did and you knew I knew . . . So how about a confession?

GEORGE: There's nothing to confess to!

HELENE: All right. Stonewall it if you want to.

GEORGE: I'm not stonewalling anything! There's nothing to stonewall. I . . . I . . . Well, I didn't know you knew.

HELENE: *(Springing up)* You had to know! Good Lord, I let signals out all over the place! That is one of the most annoying things about you. You can't pick up a signal unless I shoot a cannon across your bow.

GEORGE: Hey, wait.

HELENE: Oh, don't worry, dear, we're not fighting. Just put it down to high decibel intercourse. *(Toast)* To getting through your screwing around . . . And those sudden fits of mine. *(Clicks glasses)* Now we're a couple of lizards in brand-new skins . . . George, let's have a party! Our oldest and dearest friends, circa dating days! We'll get them out of jeans into tuxes and long dresses.

GEORGE: Sure! A sort of senior's prom. *(They begin to get comfortable in front of the fire. George is expansive, takes in the fireplace)* God, I've been dreaming about this scene ever since Keith said he was going up to Washington!

HELENE: That was a year ago.

GEORGE: Probably the longest foreplay in the history of love.

(They settle down in front of fireplace)

HELENE: Remember those films we saw in the Human Sexuality course?

GEORGE: Sure.

HELENE: You be the man, I'll be the woman. *(She lies down alongside of him, pinning his arm beneath her)*

GEORGE: Honey, my arm is under there. *(He sits up, gets a cramp in his back which he rubs out, then:)* God, there's so much to be said for the nuclear family once the electrons split off.

HELENE: Ahuh. *(Arms around him)* Hang on, George. You may hear sounds you haven't heard in thirty years.

(Upstairs, Michael comes out of his room. Does not see his parents)

HELENE: *(Suddenly alerted)* Did you hear something?

GEORGE: What?

HELENE: I don't know. I thought I heard something.

GEORGE: It's nothing.

(They go back to embracing. Michael, barefooted, comes down the stairs, crosses into kitchen, and will go to refrigerator. Helene and George do not see him)

HELENE: *(Alerted again; sotto voce)* Footsteps. I heard footsteps.

GEORGE: *(Sotto voce)* I don't hear anything.

HELENE: I tell you, someone's breathing.

GEORGE: Darling, I am. Why are you so jumpy?

HELENE: *(Tense)* I don't know.

GEORGE: Come on, honey . . .

(Refrigerator door is slammed shut by Michael)

HELENE: *(Bolts upright)* Somebody's stealing our food!

GEORGE: *(Also convinced)* God, you're right!

HELENE: *(Jumps up, pulls robe tightly around her; frantically)* I've always dreaded this! Always! A burglar when I had no clothes on!

GEORGE: *(Is on his feet also)* Whoever you are, take what you want and get out! Don't try anything funny! I'm armed, I've got a bead on you, I'll put a bullet through you . . . !

(Suddenly the lights come on, turned on by Michael who stands there with a carton of milk. George has his fingers crooked in a "gun." Which Michael looks at)

MICHAEL: Careful, Dad, it might be loaded.

GEORGE: *(Stunned)* Michael!

HELENE: *(Stunned)* Michael! *(Flustered)* But . . . but, what're you doing here? Is something wrong? *(The mother)* Oh, Michael, you look, you look awful.

MICHAEL: Yeah.

HELENE: Is Brenda with you?

MICHAEL: No, she's still taking classes. What're you guys doing? *(Observes scene, catches on)* Oh. *(Starts away as George hurriedly gets fur rug out of sight)*

HELENE: *(Immediately worried Michael may have seen)* How long have you been here?

MICHAEL: This afternoon. I didn't feel like talking to anyone.

HELENE: *(That's not what she's talking about)* How long have you been here!? Right here! In this vicinity . . . ?

GEORGE: *(Interjecting)* Did you drink the wine?

MICHAEL: Yeah.

GEORGE: The *whole* bottle?

MICHAEL: Great.

GEORGE: *(Reassuring Helene)* It's okay, honey. He didn't see anything, he was blotto.

HELENE: Are you sure?

GEORGE: Positive.

MICHAEL: *(Indicating scene of love)* Go on. Don't let me
bother you. *(Exits back toward garage)*

HELENE: He saw! My privacy lasted all of eight hours! I'm
50 years old, I'm making love in public. *(Will exit to the
bedroom to change into casual clothes)*

GEORGE: *(Trying hard to reassure her)* Honey, he didn't
see anything! Whenever have you known Michael to see
anything around him? It's a wonder he doesn't walk into
walls.

*(Offstage, in garage, a small crash to which George reacts
. . . From a hook outside patio door, George gets jogging
suit which he will put on . . . Helene reenters. Her thinking has gone beyond George's. Aware of the phenomenon
of returning kids, she is going into panic)*

HELENE: Why is he here? Why, all of a sudden, did he
appear?

GEORGE: Honey, I don't know.

HELENE: Then go to him and find out. The semester is
about to begin. Something's wrong. The last time we
saw him his beard was neatly trimmed, his hair was
styled, he wore a nice suit. Now he looks like he's been
living in the city dump. Something's wrong!

GEORGE: Please, relax. We don't know anything's
wrong . . .

HELENE: I am relaxed! . . . What's he doing here?

GEORGE: I don't know! How would I know! For God's sake, there's no reason to panic . . .

HELENE: *(The hell there isn't)* George, don't you realize what's going on these days? Bruce Adamlee came home the other day and dug in!

GEORGE: Bruce? He must be 35 years old.

HELENE: He couldn't make it on $3.35 an hour. Sally Ross is back.

GEORGE: No, no, she left again.

HELENE: She's back again. She always buys a return ticket. She uses the house as a holding depot between marriages . . . Terry Handley is back, too.

GEORGE: Stan's kid?

HELENE: The fellow he's been living with decided to go straight . . . Laurie Willard's back. With two grandchildren . . . Open your eyes! It's epidemic! It's going on all over the country! They're coming back like yo-yos.

GEORGE: Helene, please, stop making comparisons! Michael isn't gay! He's not between marriages! He's got a job earning over twenty thousand a year . . . !

HELENE: Something's wrong . . .

GEORGE: Helene, for God's sake . . .

John R. Schwandy

HELENE: Please stop calling my name! I know my name! What I don't know is how many suitcases he brought with him! *(She stops, her eyes having caught the situation map. She steps closer to it, examines it, seeing that the Michael flag has been moved to L.A.)* Never mind the suitcases. Michael's statement has been made. Boston has returned to L.A.

GEORGE: Honey, please, that doesn't mean anything! You know Michael, he's always dramatizing! He's doing research with a world-class mathematician! He's got classes to teach! He's got to go back! *(His conciliatory nature)* Now let's just see what this is all about before we jump to conclusions.

(Michael reenters carrying box of lab equipment: flasks, retorts, etc.)

GEORGE: *(Expansively)* Well, son, this is a nice surprise! Good to see you!

MICHAEL: Good to see you too, Dad. You too, Mom. Thanks for those socks you sent me.

HELENE: *(About box Michael brought in: bit of suspicion)* What's all that?

MICHAEL: Oh, just some of my life-science stuff. Where's Keith?

HELENE: *(Some forbearance; knows her son)* Michael, we wrote you. He's gone up to the University of Washington.

MICHAEL: Oh, yeah. That's right. Elliott?

HELENE: Elliott doesn't live here anymore. He's married.

MICHAEL: He is? . . . Oh, that's right! He married Karen and they live in Dallas.

HELENE: He married Nancy and they live in Dallas.

MICHAEL: *(Beat as he ponders this)* Nancy? Are you sure?

HELENE: Well, we can always check with Elliott. That's all right, son. You got half of it right.

GEORGE: *(Feeling things out)* Well, son, how are things in Cambridge? We thought you'd be getting ready for the new semester now.

MICHAEL: Yeah, that's what they think too.

GEORGE: *(Some suspicion now himself)* Why aren't you preparing for the new semester?

MICHAEL: No point. I'm quitting.

(George and Helene exchange glances)

HELENE: You're quitting what?

MICHAEL: MIT.

GEORGE: *(Astounded)* You're quitting the Massachusetts Institute of Technology!? I don't understand. It's practically impossible to get a good college teaching job these days. You've got the best, the most prestigious university in the country . . .

MICHAEL: It's the pits.

GEORGE: *(The pits? Stunned)* MIT??

MICHAEL: Men in Trouble. Dad, it's all a con. Government
pumps in the bread. The Good Ole Boy System, East
Coast style.

GEORGE: Son, this is serious. You've got a contract. You
break your contract there you'll never get another math
job in any university. For God's sake, think a minute.
This is a life decision.

MICHAEL: *(Unperturbed)* Yeah, I can see that all right.
(Heads for stairs with table)

HELENE: *(About his quitting MIT)* But why, Michael?

MICHAEL: The pits.

GEORGE: *(That's unfathomable)* Cambridge? Cambridge,
Massachusetts? Boston!? It's a great American city . . .

MICHAEL: The pits. It's one huge combat zone. And the
weather in winter! Dad, they've got *blizzards*. The only
time I saw the sun was when I opened an astronomy
book.

GEORGE: Okay, I can understand that. A California kid,
you're not used to . . .

MICHAEL: Bottom of my car rusted out. You know why?
They *salt* their roads. In L.A. we season our lettuce, in
Boston they season the asphalt.

GEORGE: There's a very good reason for that . . .

MICHAEL: If they do have a leash law, nobody pays attention to it. You've got to walk along, hunched over to avoid the land mines. Stuff freezes up, kids use them for pucks in street hockey.

GEORGE: Now I know you're making half of this up! Michael, what is it? What's the real problem there?

MICHAEL: *(Especially deeply felt)* Dad, it's an unfriendly, uptight place! Once in a while you get a "hi" back. I plotted it. The ratio of "hi's" out to "hi's" back is fourteen to one.

HELENE: But what about Professor Neumann and the research? He's depending on you.

MICHAEL: Mom, I doubt he even knows I'm gone. He sits in his apartment, shades down, a desk lamp on, doing math days running. He doesn't even know if it's day or night outside. That isolation. It's typical of mathematicians. I asked him once if he ever went to plays or concerts. He never goes, he says, he'd rather imagine them. I don't want to be like that, so removed from everything. *(Starts taking table upstairs)*

HELENE: Why are you taking that upstairs?

MICHAEL: I'm setting up my lab. I'm dumping math.

GEORGE: You're what? But you just got your doctorate.

MICHAEL: I've decided it's not for me.

GEORGE: After nine years!?

MICHAEL: Dad, nobody cares about math. No one can even understand it. The umbral calculus. Do you even know what it means?

GEORGE: I don't have to know what it means. I'm an accountant.

MICHAEL: But you know about genetic engineering. Okay, that's where the funding is. I'm switching to life science. I can pick up a degree in no time.

HELENE: And how long is no time?

MICHAEL: Oh, three, four years.

HELENE: I see. *(Hopefully)* So you'll get yourself a nice little place near school . . .

MICHAEL: Mom, I can't take on any more expense. I've still got my share of the Cambridge apartment.

GEORGE: You mean you'll go to UCLA here and pay rent at MIT there. Michael, you must be a genius, I don't understand you at all.

MICHAEL: Work out fine, Dad. I don't mind living here in the slightest.

HELENE: *(A last try)* Brenda! Oh, Michael, she's such a lovely girl. You'll miss her something awful!

MICHAEL: Not if I can get her to come here too. *(Enters his room)*

HELENE: Now can I panic?

GEORGE: Wait for me, we'll start together.

HELENE: He's so big. Did you see how big he is?

GEORGE: Well, he's no seven, that's for sure. The best he is
is a stretched-out four. *(His conciliatory explanation of
Michael)* Culture trauma. A California kid's too soft. The
East is harder . . .

HELENE: So, shell-shocked, the trooper returns to the san-
itarium.

GEORGE: Well, it's not all his fault.

HELENE: *(Firmly)* No, George, it's ours.

GEORGE: Ours?

HELENE: Of course it is! He didn't like grad school in Ore-
gon, it was too wet. He didn't like New Mexico, it was
too dry. MIT's too cold, Florida's too hot. We didn't raise
a person, we raised a citrus fruit. *(The guilts of child
rearing are setting in)* We made it too easy for him. We
didn't want to hurt him, we didn't want to offend him,
we didn't want to . . . *(Hates that word) frustrate* him
. . . !

GEORGE: Of course we didn't! What's so great about frustration? Freud said . . .

HELENE: No. The Co-op school said Freud said and parents never learned to say "no."

GEORGE: No! We said "no" a hundred times! I remember
it very clearly. "No, Michael," I said . . .

HELENE: *(Going right on)* Paula Benedict's kid didn't want to be in his bedroom. He wanted to be in the living room. How did he get there? He chopped his way through the wall! Did they take his hatchet away? No, they praised him for his ingenuity! . . . Wilma's kid, 6 years old, ran around naked all the time, playing with himself. Did anybody stop him? No! All they did was comment on how well he was hung!

GEORGE: Helene, for God's sake, you are blowing this out of all proportions . . . !

HELENE: George, I don't want to fight about this . . .

GEORGE: *(Very agitated)* We are not fighting!

(Helene is angry and, of course, a lot of it is self-directed for "not having known better")

HELENE: It was dumb times and we were just as dumb as anybody! We were chicken, frightened of our own child, afraid he wouldn't love us! We cheated him out of building self-confidence. We never taught him to face *into* a problem, now he runs from them! . . . It all goes back to that shovel.

GEORGE: *(That's a baffling turn)* What shovel?

HELENE: Philip! Every time Michael reached down to pick up the marbles, Philip stepped on his hand!

GEORGE: Oh, that creepy kid next door.

HELENE: Don't you remember? Michael got a shovel, reared back to belt the bully, and *you* stopped him!

GEORGE: *(Astonished she'd even question that)* Of course I stopped him!

HELENE: You shouldn't have!

GEORGE: What are you talking about? He could have killed the kid!

HELENE: I doubt it. Philip was wearing a tin suit.

GEORGE: I don't remember a tin suit.

HELENE: Yes, he was dressed up to play in *The Wizard of Oz.*

GEORGE: No, you are mistaken.

HELENE: I am not mistaken.

GEORGE: I'm sorry, you are.

HELENE: I'm sorry, I'm not.

(George is on his feet and the heat of the conflict grows)

GEORGE: Okay, okay, Spock covered that in his book! Do not let your kid belt the neighbor's kid with a shovel even if he is playing in *The Wizard of Oz!* This is incredible! What are you doing?

HELENE: I am only pointing out that that was a critical time in Michael's development . . .

GEORGE: You are dredging up something that took place twenty years ago! Good God, have you been harboring resentment all these years I stifled Michael's killer instinct at age 10?

HELENE: *(Flustered)* Oh, I don't know what I'm doing! But I do know Michael is going to be upstairs doing those experiments of his. Have you forgotten? The house smelled like the tar pits.

GEORGE: The kid was only giving expression to his active, inquisitive mind!

HELENE: The kid was pouring acid down the pot! We had the only toilet bowl in the city that smoked!

GEORGE: But he was only a kid then! He didn't know what he was doing!

HELENE: He is giving up a once-in-a-lifetime opportunity at the most prestigious university in the whole country. Do you think he knows what he's doing now!?

(That stops George)

GEORGE: Yeah. Something's going on back there, that's for sure. You know how secretive Michael can be. Well, I'm going to find out what it is . . . My God, when we left home we wouldn't dream of coming back except to visit! We were independent! . . . Fantastic. Try to do the right thing. Work hard, get a nice house, put in a pool, stuff the refrigerator. Draws them back like bees to honey.

(To Helene this is a critical moment. And she knows that to get what she wants, she has to handle George gently)

HELENE: George, this is a critical moment. We want him to change, we have to change too. We have to be tougher.

GEORGE: Let the kid know how things stand.

HELENE: Please stop calling him "kid." He is not a kid! He is 30 years old. That's halfway to retirement. He is healthy. He's bright.

GEORGE: Oh, God knows he's bright. He speaks three languages. He's a gourmet cook. He can play chess blindfolded . . .

HELENE: So never mind saying "no" to him a hundred times. Go upstairs and say "no" to him once.

GEORGE: Okay, okay, you're right. I'll talk to him. *(Cranking up for a confrontation with Michael, he starts to the stairs. Helene follows)*

HELENE: George, you've got to be very careful what you say to Michael. You know he knows everything. And don't get into history whatever you do. He'll take you back to a generation when nobody ever left home.

GEORGE: Yeah. Cool. Matter-of-fact. He can make his own life choices. We're behind him. But at his age he cannot stay here indefinitely . . . Would you like to come up with me?

HELENE: We're a traditional family. I did the socks. You do this.

*(She exits. George goes up the stairs to Michael's room . . .
As he gets to the door and knocks, Michael comes flying
out, thrusting kung fu short swords)*

MICHAEL: Eyes . . . throat . . . bladder.

*(George retreats down the stairs. Michael moves along af-
ter him, wielding the swords)*

Kung Fu . . . I had to learn it. *(More sword thrusts)* If you
ever went shopping in Filene's basement you'd know
what I mean. *(Lunges)* Eyes . . . throat . . . bladder.

GEORGE: That's very graceful.

MICHAEL: It started as dance, you know. It was only much
later that it became a martial art. *(Lunges)*

GEORGE: I see. Michael, I have to talk to you.

MICHAEL: *(Continuing his exercises)* Sure.

GEORGE: Could you put those blades away, son? I'd feel
more comfortable if you weren't armed.

MICHAEL: Oh, sure. *(Will put short swords away, eat
cheese, drink milk)* Oh, incidentally, if Professor Neumann calls, tell him I'm not here. I don't want to talk to
him.

GEORGE: Are you having some difficulty with him?

MICHAEL: No.

GEORGE: I see. That's why you don't want to talk to him?
Michael, what's going on back there . . . ?

MICHAEL: *(Evading it)* Dad, what'd you want to talk to me about?

GEORGE: Son, we have a little problem here.

MICHAEL: Then I'm glad I'm home. Maybe I can help out.

GEORGE: Yes, well . . .

MICHAEL: You and Mom okay?

GEORGE: Oh, sure, we're fine.

MICHAEL: Well, I'm okay too. Don't worry about me. Sure is great to see the old room again. I did some real good math up there in the old days.

GEORGE: Yes, I remember. Michael . . .

MICHAEL: Sure is great to see your face and Mom's. You don't know how good it is, Dad, to be able to come back. Most guys can't. Their parents don't want them. Fantastic feeling to know there's always a place for me and people who love me.

(This, of course, is not what George needs to help him "confront" Michael)

GEORGE: Oh, we love you, son. We certainly do.

MICHAEL: I know, I can really feel it. Oh, Boston's okay, I guess. But mostly it was just plain lonely. Until I met Brenda, seems I was alone all the time.

GEORGE: Yeah, well that's not much fun.

MICHAEL: Well? . . . The problem you've been having.

GEORGE: Hmm? Oh, that. We'll talk about it later. Go on, finish your exercises.

MICHAEL: You sure?

GEORGE: Sure. Look, your mother's a little on edge, she's trying to work something out, so be careful, huh?

MICHAEL: Oh, sure, sure.

(He goes to his room with swords, milk cartons, etc. George calls to Helene in their bedroom)

GEORGE: Honey . . .

(Helene enters. From George's look, she realizes what happened)

HELENE: You didn't tell him.

GEORGE: I tried. I couldn't. He misses us, he's lonely. It won't be so bad. *(Selling her)* Look, we can work it out. He doesn't have to do his experiments upstairs; he can do them in the dressing room out back. We'll set firm ground rules . . .

HELENE: George, you haven't been listening to a thing I said. I was planning on using the dressing room myself. I was going to turn it into a studio and work there.

GEORGE: Oh, yeah, Ralph's gallery. *(An idea)* Keith's room! You can work up there! It's got a perfect north . . . east light. Honey, it'll work out fine! You'll paint up a storm! Won't be long we'll all be heading for the valley and a one-woman show!

(In spite of herself Helene smiles)

HELENE: You're the great conciliator, aren't you, George? Yes, I've always loved that about you . . . Well, maybe it won't be too bad. After all, Michael isn't in the hospital, he's not in jail, he's not into drugs . . . all he is is upstairs.

GEORGE: That's the spirit!

HELENE: *(Has made her accommodation)* Come on, let's drink our wine, sit in front . . .

(The front door flies open. In comes Elliott, the Butler middle son from Dallas. He wears a neatly tailored Western suit, bolo tie, boots. He holds two suitcases and is in a foul mood. About Elliott: A "charmer." He is very much self-involved, but in a different way than Michael. He works in sales, is comfortable with hype, and has his own sense of logic. He is constantly on the move, "doing, planning." When he crosses a mirror, he checks his appearance—hair, tie, brushes lint off clothes—and does isometrics. As far as playing a scene with Elliott: only when he himself wants to)

HELENE: . . . Elliott!

ELLIOTT: *(Grumbling)* Hi, Mom.

HELENE: Elliott, what are you doing here? What happened?

ELLIOTT: Nothing! Nothing happened! Not one damn thing!

GEORGE: Son, son . . .

(But Elliott has dumped his things and exits)

HELENE: Is Nancy with him? Can you see?

GEORGE: *(Peering out door)* I don't see her.

(Elliott is back in with more stuff)

HELENE: Elliott, is Nancy with you? Is she all right?

ELLIOTT: She's fine! She's great! She just threw me out, that's all! I come home, all my clothes are on the front lawn! Shirts, underwear, pants . . . and she didn't even fold them, for Christ's sake! *(He's out again)*

HELENE: Good Lord, another shell-shocked trooper.

GEORGE: *(As Elliott returns with the last of his things)* But what did she say?

ELLIOTT: Nothing! Not one damn thing! "I don't want to be married," she said. "I don't feel comfortable having my space invaded." Her space invaded, for Christ's sake!

HELENE: *(Knows her son)* Elliott, what did you do?

ELLIOTT: Me? *Me!?* Nothing! Not one damn thing! If Dad came to you and apologized for something he did, you'd accept it, wouldn't you?

HELENE: Well, yes, I suppose so.

ELLIOTT: There! Of course you would! That's the kind of person you are . . . Ah, the hell with it. Lots of women around, plenty of them, just dying to have their space invaded.

(Drawn by the voices, Michael comes out of his room)

MICHAEL: Elliott! *(Comes downstairs)*

ELLIOTT: Michael!

(They slap hands. The brothers like each other. Helene and George look on in stunned amazement)

ELLIOTT: What're you doing here?

MICHAEL: Scratching MIT. Going back to UCLA.

ELLIOTT: All right! You back up in your room?

MICHAEL: Yeah.

ELLIOTT: Me, too! Fantastic! Be like old times. Hey, we ought to get Keith back down, reunite the old terror squad.

MICHAEL: Really!

ELLIOTT: Come on, give me a hand. *(They start gathering Elliott's things)* You shaved your beard.

MICHAEL: Yeah, I'm in revolt.

ELLIOTT: Me, too! I'm thinking of putting one on.

HELENE: *(Trying)* Elliott, what about your job back there?

ELLIOTT: No problem, Mom. I'm on stress leave. *(He goes into his bedroom with his load. Michael hangs back)*

MICHAEL: What happened?

GEORGE: Nancy threw him out.

MICHAEL: Oh. He should have married Karen. *(Michael goes into Elliott's room with his load)*

HELENE: We didn't raise sons, we raised homing pigeons. Well, it's our fault too, you know. Elliott coming back.

GEORGE: Helene, please, don't start that again.

HELENE: It is. Self-reliance. We hurt him there too. We did massive ego damage. We were too hard on him.

GEORGE: I see. We were too easy on Michael and too hard on Elliott.

HELENE: Yes. We recognized our mistake with the first one . . .

GEORGE: And made up for it by making the opposite mistake with the second one. I'm sorry, you're a mother, but you can't have it both ways.

HELENE: But that's what happened.

GEORGE: *(Forcefully)* No, that is not what happened! We were fantastic parents! We were loving, considerate, giving, attentive, wise! In grade school we gave up an NCAA championship game—*(It still galls him)*—the greatest college basketball ever played—to see Elliott in

Billy Goat Gruff. As parents we were perfect, but were done in by evil forces!

HELENE: What are you talking about?

GEORGE: *(His outrage)* The Sixties, goddamn them! *(Mocking)* "Get high, get it off, hey, man, come on, let's get our shit together." Why any sane person'd want it all gathered in one place is beyond me! . . . Now *that* was a real dumb time! No wonder Henry's kid can't make more than $3.35 an hour. He was so busy screwing around with his hair he never even learned how to make change! . . . Face it, honey, what we are catching is fallout. Our sons are just a couple of droplets in the acid rain.

HELENE: I don't want them here. I feel guilty, I feel self-ish, and I resent feeling that way. Oh, I'm so confused. It's not fair, I've done my time. I thought by now I didn't have to be a parent anymore. I could become an ordinary person. Oh, why aren't people like bears? At a certain age, run them up a tree. By the time they come down, Mama's split.

GEORGE: Yes, but what bear gets to take grandchildren to Disneyland?

HELENE: I know, you want to smooth things over . . . but, George, this is different. I need some help here. I was 18 years old. I had a full scholarship to the Art Institute. My mural took the blue ribbon at the Young Artists' League. My mother said after I got married, I'd forget all that. My job would be to become a wife and mother. She also said I'd get fat.

GEORGE: You didn't get fat.

HELENE: Yes, I did defy something, didn't I? I had talent, it's still there. I've got something to say. Oh, maybe not earthshaking, but I want to paint life's good things. There are some, you know. There are yellows and oranges, they're all around . . .

GEORGE: You'll do it, you'll see!

(To this point this is the most assertive Helene has been, but there's more plea to it than force)

HELENE: George, the battlefield's right here. This is our turf and you've got to let them know.

GEORGE: I will, I'll make it very clear. We'll meet them part way, but we call the shots.

HELENE: First thing in the morning I'm going to the beach. I'm going to take dozens of photos. I'm going to paint my pictures and astound the art world even if it's only in the valley. *(Takes bottle of wine, starts for yard)*

GEORGE: Where are you going?

HELENE: Back into the hot tub. Come on, George, I need you to hold my head up out of the water.

LIGHTS OUT

Scene 3

The same. A few days later. Late afternoon going to evening. Phones have been brought in for Michael and Elliott. At his room, Elliott works with hammer and nails putting up posters, turning his place into a bachelor's pad. Michael is at his room with his phone. Downstairs something new has been added to a central location: a standard holding three colored lights, red, green, and white. Each light is now off. By the standard, George works with screwdriver.

GEORGE: *(Calling up)* Okay, Michael, ring Elliott's number!

(Michael rings Elliott's number. Elliott's phone rings. At the same time the green light on the bank of lights begins to blink on and off. Elliott stops what he's doing and answers the phone. Green light stops blinking, stays on)

ELLIOTT: Howdy.

MICHAEL: *(Into phone)* Me. Just testing the lights. Hang up now and ring my number.

ELLIOTT: You do it. I'm busy.

MICHAEL: I can't ring my own number!

(But Elliott has already hung up and gone back to work in his room. Green light off)

Dad, ring my number!

GEORGE: Right!

(On living room phone George rings Michael's number. Red light blinks on and off until Michael answers)

MICHAEL: *(Seeing it works)* Hey, all right!

GEORGE: Okay, ring me.

(Michael hangs up, red light off. Michael rings number. White light goes on and off . . . Helene, wearing an artist's smock and carrying paintbrushes, runs in. The pressure of "family" life has been building in her. She and George each answer a phone)

HELENE/GEORGE: Hello! . . . Hello!

GEORGE: *(Over phone)* It's all right, dear. Just checking out the phones.

(Helene, upset, hangs up. She will cross to sink to clean her brushes. George has been taking charge, his way)

Great! That should handle which phone is ringing. Now all we've got to do is keep ourselves in light bulbs.

(Michael has come down, crossed his parents, and exited to patio. Meanwhile, green light has gone on, indicating Elliott is making a call in his room)

(To Helene) Oh, I've got a call in to Professor Neumann. I'm going to find out what that's all about with Michael and straighten it out.

HELENE: Good luck!

(George picks up the tools he has been working with and exits to the garage. Elliott, meanwhile, appears in his doorway, holding phone but getting no answer)

ELLIOTT: Damn! She's there, I know she's there, just not answering! *(Hangs up. Comes down. Will get a beer out of the refrigerator)* Oh, hell, Mom, I don't want to break up. Marriages need work to hold them together, isn't that right?

HELENE: Well, yes . . .

(Another characteristic of Elliott: he always thinks he's right)

ELLIOTT: Sure! Problem comes up, couples have to work it through . . . There was this office party. Okay. I got a little high, maybe I shouldn't have. Lisa was there, she works sales with me. She threw it, I caught; maybe I shouldn't have. But it didn't mean anything. Lisa means nothing to me, zilch! I don't even like her, Mom, she's got a square ass. You know I don't like women with square asses.

HELENE: No, Elliott, I don't believe you've shared that information.

(Michael plods in, carrying package, goes to phone, and rings number)

ELLIOTT: Well, Nancy sure knows it. *(Heads upstairs with beer)* Okay, I did the mature thing. I apologized. "Nancy," I said, "I'm sorry, I'm very sorry about Lisa" . . . Hell, I even told her I was sorry about Joyce, too.

(He's back in his room. Helene is looking up at him, knowing now why Nancy was pissed. Helene will listen to Michael's conversation and react)

MICHAEL: Hi, Brenda, did Professor Neumann call? *(Devastated)* He didn't even call! Not once! Not even to find out if I'm living or dead! . . . I know I don't want to talk to him, I want him to want to talk to me . . . No . . . No, I'm not working on the math problem. What's the point? I'm working on my multiplication tables instead. I'm up to my twelvesies . . . I'm missing you a lot . . . Then come on out. Check the law schools here . . . *Here.* You'll love it. Plenty of room, pool, hot tub, my folks are great . . . Sure, bring the dog.

(Big reaction from Helene) Yeah, all right. *(Hangs up, sees his mother)* She doesn't want to come.

HELENE: Oh, what a shame.

MICHAEL: *(As he starts for stairs with bundle)* It's okay, Mom, I'm working on her.

HELENE: Michael, what have you got on the stove?

MICHAEL: Warming up some tomato sauce.

HELENE: For a meal or are you working on an experiment?

MICHAEL: Eggplant parmigiana.

HELENE: I'd appreciate it if you didn't do dinner in here the same time you're doing an experiment out there.

MICHAEL: No problem, Mom. I just bought this.

(Casually holds up fire extinguisher. Phone rings, activating white light. Eyes to light. George comes running back in. Helene is flustered)

HELENE: Which color is ours?

GEORGE: White! We're white, Helene, that's for us.

(Helene heads for phone muttering "white, white" as:)

MICHAEL: *(From landing)* If it's Professor Neumann I don't want to talk to him!

HELENE: *(Answers phone)* Hello . . . What? . . . No, I'm sorry, you have the wrong color. *(Bangs down phone, fuming)*

GEORGE: *(Reading her)* You all right?

HELENE: Outstanding!

GEORGE: Just wondering. You have the look of someone about to shoot a cannon across a number of bows.

HELENE: My, George, what progress you're making! *(Hammering from Elliott's room. Her litany)* I'm ignoring it. I'm ignoring all that's going on around here. I'm above it. I'm my own person, I'm a horse with blinkers. *(More hammering from Elliott's room)* I know I'm ignoring it, but what's going on up there?

GEORGE: Reconstruction. Plans by *Playboy*.

HELENE: I see. The girls are going to start parading through. Too bad. I like Nancy, she's first-rate. I thought maybe she could settle him down. You know what happened between them? Elliott's been chasing again.

GEORGE: Yeah, that's what I thought. I wish there was something we could do.

HELENE: I don't know what short of tying it off. He's such a juvenile.

GEORGE: He's 28.

HELENE: I'm afraid he won't be 28 until he's 38. I would like to talk to him. His behavior toward Nancy is rotten.

GEORGE: Hang out by the refrigerator. You'll catch him coming in to refuel.

HELENE: Oh, there's another problem, the refrigerator. Elliott put a whole case of beer in it. It can't hold that and all of Michael's organic vegetables. I'd like to ignore it, but every time I open the door a red cabbage rolls out.

GEORGE: Don't worry. I'll repair the spare fridge and put it on the service porch.

HELENE: That's cluttered as is.

GEORGE: No problem. I'll have it uncluttered! *(Green light goes on indicating Elliott is on phone in his room)* And the rain gutters cleared. And the facia painted. The work'll be good for them. Besides, I think it is up to us to create an atmosphere around here they will find repellent.

(Michael comes out of his room carrying a steaming pan and goes into the bathroom)

GEORGE: *(Glance at watch)* I'm going to try Professor Neumann again. *(Goes to phone to dial . . .)*

HELENE: *(Calling Elliott in his bedroom)* Elliott . . . Elliott!

(Elliott comes out of his room on tail end of phone conversation. Not wanting Elliott to hear his conversation about Michael, George takes phone out to patio)

ELLIOTT: *(On phone)* Okay, okay, Wally, now what about the merchandise? . . . The packaging? . . . All right! . . . Hey, that's the great thing about a mail-order business, I can run it from the house.

(Helene, heading for her bedroom, is brought up short)

ELLIOTT: Right! *(Elliott hangs up, comes downstairs to get some food)*

HELENE: What was that?

ELLIOTT: Mail-order racket, Mom. Big bucks to be made. Hey, that's an idea. Want to team up?

(Oblivious to the others, Michael comes down to go to stove and get his eggplant parmigiana)

ELLIOTT: We were in business before, remember? *(As she doesn't)* The lemonade stand!

HELENE: Elliott, you were 8 years old!

ELLIOTT: Yeah, we made a hell of a unit, huh, cutie? How about it? I'll make you VP.

HELENE: No, thanks. *(Starts to broach a subject)* Elliott . . .

(Michael is crossing with his tray of food. Elliott pokes into the pan)

ELLIOTT: Hey, whatcha got there?

MICHAEL: Cyanide patties.

(Elliott pulls his hand away quickly. Michael goes up to his room. Meanwhile)

HELENE: Elliott, will you please sit down, I want to talk to you about Nancy . . .

ELLIOTT: *(He "understands"; interrupts)* Yeah, I know. Worries me too. Look, I'm trying to hold it together. I'm trying to be understanding and sympathetic, like Dad would be. I pointed out to her young couples often have trouble in the beginning. She seemed to grab that. I suggested therapy. She seemed to grab that too. "All right," I said, *"you* can start going right away." . . . Damm near decked me with the iron. *(In his mind, he's the one beset upon!)* Hard to figure, Mom. Real hard. Guess you're the last of the reasonable females. *(Green light and phone rings)* Green.

(Elliott runs up to his room. George returns from the patio with phone, having talked to Professor Neumann. Helene, having been buffeted pretty good, is beginning to let go)

HELENE: George, this is not going to work! I'm having a great deal of trouble with Elliott's thought processes. *(She will move about removing smock, getting sweater and purse to leave house; she's wound up)* There is a definite disadvantage knowing too much about your children . . . especially when they're shitheads . . . Well, I've decided! I am going to get a studio at the beach! I will leave this zoo every morning at eight! I will return every evening and throw them raw meat! . . . Not that I like the idea! No, I do not, not one bit! It feels as though I am being driven out of my own house . . . !

GEORGE: Helene, I just talked to Professor Neumann. He told me what happened with Michael.

HELENE: *(Which stops her)* What?

GEORGE: For his research project Michael wanted to take on a problem some great math minds had worked on and failed to solve. Professor Neumann told him not to, that it was too hard. You know Michael: That's all he had to hear. He took it on anyway, worked on it through the first semester, vowing he would solve it. He worked on it through the second semester, vowing he would solve it. He didn't solve it. Now he's got egg on his face. The year's gone by, he's got nothing to show for it. He's dumping MIT before they dump him . . . I don't know what to do about it.

HELENE: *(Sudden enlightenment)* George, we don't have to do anything about it.

GEORGE: What do you mean?

HELENE: Michael blew it, let *him* do something about it.

GEORGE: We've got to be helpful.

HELENE: What are you going to do? Study math for nine years and solve the problem for him? . . . I thought we agreed to change.

GEORGE: We are, but we still have some responsibility as parents.

HELENE: Good God, someday responsibility ends!

GEORGE: Yes, someday, but today is not the day!

HELENE: Oh, bullshit!

GEORGE: What is this!?

HELENE: Filthy language, if I'm not mistaken!

GEORGE: I've never seen you this way!

HELENE: I know. Fuck, fuck, fuck. That's me!

GEORGE: That is not you! I know you! You are . . . you are . . . *(Sudden realization; stunned)* Helene . . . We're fighting!

HELENE: Thank God, I never thought you'd recognize it!

GEORGE: I'm sorry, I . . .

(Suddenly, in dressing room out back, there is an explosion casting smoke and fumes. Everybody reacts. The house alarm system goes off. George runs out to see what happened. On phone Michael says he'll call back, grabs fire extinguisher, races down. Elliott races down)

HELENE: *(To Michael as he goes by)* What is it?

MICHAEL: It's not the eggplant parmigiana!

(Michael runs outside, sprays the fire extinguisher. Elliott runs out also with movie camera)

GEORGE: *(Sticks his head in)* Holy Christ! It blew part of the dressing room into the hot tub!

(Vanishes again as: minor pandemonium out back. Michael sprays the fire extinguisher. Ad libs: "It's okay, it's out, it's not serious." But smoke and fumes still float in)

MICHAEL: *(Sticks his head in)* Sorry, Mom. I just didn't get the reaction I expected. *(Vanishes again)*

ELLIOTT: *(Sticks his head in)* Wow! The bougainvillea's turned black! *(Holds up camera)* Film at eleven! *(Vanishes again)*

GEORGE: *(Coming in)* Okay, it's all under control. Nobody got hurt . . .

HELENE: That settles it! There will be no more experiments around the house . . . !

GEORGE: Now, Helene, please, don't have one of your fits. It's okay.

HELENE: I am not having a fit and it is not okay!

GEORGE: *(The Great Conciliator sees the positive side)* Sure! Don't you see? You won't need a studio at the beach anymore! The dressing room out there now has a natural north light! See, everything's working out fine!

(Door chimes sound. Draws Helene's and George's attention)

HELENE: *(A horrible premonition)* It's Keith coming back
. . . I know it! I just know it!

(George opens the front door. In comes Janie Johnson, an effervescent and adorable 18-year-old, carrying her belongings. Janie is the type of person who sees the bright side of everything)

JANIE: *(As though they would know)* Hi! I'm Janie!

(The Butlers look puzzled)

You know, Janie Johnson! Oh, this is awfully nice of you,
Mr. and Mrs. Butler. I didn't have the slightest idea what
I was going to do!

HELENE: Do we have a child I don't know about?

(George is equally puzzled, which Janie observes)

JANIE: Didn't Keith phone you?

GEORGE: No.

JANIE: He said he would! Oh, this is terrible! I feel so
embarrassed!

GEORGE: About what? What is this?

JANIE: *(Anguishing)* I'm going to Santa Monica College. I
couldn't get housing, I enrolled so late. Keith said his
room was empty, that I could have it for a while, that
you two were great, you wouldn't mind. Oh, I feel awful!

Don Howard, Janis Paige, Alexandra Gersten, Kevin McCarthy, Kevin O'Rourke

Alexandra Gersten, Kevin McCarthy

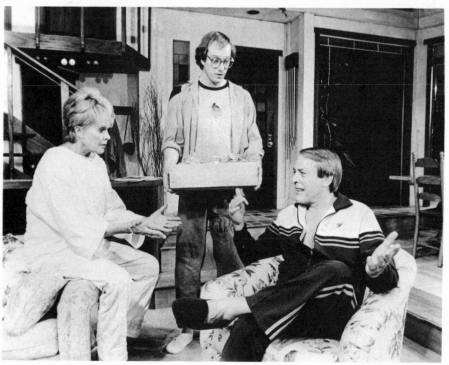

Janis Paige, Don Howard, Kevin McCarthy

Janis Paige

HELENE: I see.

(Elliott and Michael, carrying some effects of the explosion, have come in on Janie's speech)

JANIE: *(Gathering her things)* It's okay, I'll go, I've got a sleeping bag, I can sleep in the park, or in some doorway . . . !

(With Elliott, it's like radar. He crosses to Janie)

ELLIOTT: Hi.

JANIE: Hi.

ELLIOTT: I'm Elliott, Keith's brother. This is Mike, our *old* brother. *(Making sure she gets this. Michael goes up the stairs)*

JANIE: Hi.

MICHAEL: Hi.

ELLIOTT: He's a professor of mathematics. *(Gestures Michael is way out)* Well, come on, let me help you with your things. Your room's right upstairs.

(Janie's eyes go to Helene for permission. There is such a needy quality about Janie. Helene pantomimes confusion, then gestures acceptance)

HELENE: Welcome to Halfway House. You can register later.

JANIE: Gee, thanks! Thank you so much! It's only temporary! You have no idea how grateful I am! *(She stops, sniffs. Then, to Elliott)* You got a cesspool?

ELLIOTT: No, nothing like that.

JANIE: Does it always stink around here?

ELLIOTT: Only when the professor is home. Want to see my room? Here, have a sip of brewski.

(Elliott has taken Janie into his room. Michael carries Janie's things into her room)

HELENE: Well, we gave birth to three, now we have four. I think we're losing ground.

GEORGE: She must be an old friend of Keith's. Funny, I don't remember him ever mentioning her.

(Phone rings. The white light is activated. Helene answers)

JANIE: *(Upstairs; on exiting Elliott's room)* Hey, this is neat!

ELLIOTT: You're right next door. *(Leads her into Keith's room)*

HELENE: *(On phone)* Hello . . . Yes, I'll accept . . . Keith! . . . She's here already! You should have called! . . . Keith, you should have checked first! It was a very inconsiderate thing to do! . . . What? . . . Yes, dear . . . Yes, dear . . . I see. *(Relents)* All right, we'll work it out, but she can only stay a short while . . . All right, 'bye. *(She hangs up, turns to George)* She's an old friend all right. He met her yesterday in San Francisco.

GEORGE: Great.

HELENE: Apparently she was on a Wilderness Survival Course with Dave. Keith says she's into Doomsday.

GEORGE: She's come to the right place.

HELENE: Kids! When they're little, they're so cute you want to eat them up. When they grow up you wish you had!

LIGHTS OUT
CURTAIN

ACT TWO

ACT TWO

Scene 1

Before curtain rises we hear the music of the 1812 Overture.

At rise: A few days later. Michael, wearing chef's hat and vigorously swinging a baton, stands center stage conducting the music which is very, very loud.

George and Helene, carrying groceries for their party, enter from outside.

GEORGE: My God! My God! *(Shouts)* Michael! Tone down the music! *(He isn't heard)* Michael! For God's sake, the music!

MICHAEL: *(Still conducting)* What? Did you say something, Dad?

GEORGE: The music!

MICHAEL: What about it?

(Meanwhile, Helene has had enough. She crosses, turns the music off completely, exits outside to get more groceries. Michael, meanwhile, is left holding a useless baton)

God! You can't do anything around here! *(Exits to his room.
Janie, scantily-clad, as is her way, bounces out of her
room)*

JANIE: Hi, Mr. Butler!

GEORGE: Hi.

*(Janie giggles, wiggles, goes to Michael's door, knocks, goes
in. Which George sees before he exits to yard. Elliott comes
out of his room, primps. Goes to Janie's room, sees she's not
in. Looks at Michael's door, goes to it, knocks. Michael
opens door)*

ELLIOTT: Hi.

MICHAEL: Hi. *(As Elliott tries to peer around him, blocks
his view)* What's your problem?

ELLIOTT: What's happening?

MICHAEL: What's it to you?

ELLIOTT: I like her, that's what.

MICHAEL: So? You like the mannequin in Saks's window.
(Starts to shut door)

ELLIOTT: Hey, come on, give me a break.

MICHAEL: May I remind you, brother, you are still a married man.

ELLIOTT: You're living with Brenda. Philosophically it's
the same thing.

MICHAEL: I'm not a philosopher, I'm a mathematician.

(Michael shuts door on Elliott, who grumbles, goes into his room. Downstairs, Helene comes in with more groceries, goes into kitchen as George comes in from patio)

GEORGE: *(Calling up)* Michael! Michael!

MICHAEL: *(Sticking head out of bedroom)* Yeah?

GEORGE: Could you come down please and help set up the tables outside?

MICHAEL: Can't right now! I'm busy! *(Vanishes back inside)*

HELENE: What's he so busy at?

GEORGE: I'd rather not know.

HELENE: Is Janie in with him?

GEORGE: Yeah. Honey, you have to talk to her.

HELENE: George! Please, I told you I would. At the right moment.

GEORGE: I know it's an emergency and we want to be helpful . . .

HELENE: She knows she can't stay. She's looking. But she is grateful and she is trying to be helpful.

GEORGE: Yeah, I went into the bathroom after she cleaned it. There was no noticeable change.

HELENE: *(Is sympathetic toward Janie)* Well, she hasn't learned her way around a house very well.

GEORGE: She knows where the bedrooms are.

HELENE: George, I've got to have some help.

GEORGE: Yeah. *(Calling up)* Elliott! Elliott!

ELLIOTT: *(Sticks his head out his door)* Yeah?

GEORGE: Would you come down please and help with the tables?

(Elliott just stands there)

GEORGE: Elliott, did you hear me?

ELLIOTT: Yeah, I'm thinking about it.

GEORGE: What's there to think about? I asked you to do something.

ELLIOTT: *(Lightly, his joke)* Okay, okay, Dad, I agree to the exploitation. *(Starts downstairs, heads for phone)* Tote that barge, lift that bale . . . Hey, Mom, you look real deluxe today.

HELENE: Thank you, Elliott.

ELLIOTT: Gee, Dad, to keep up with her I'm afraid you're going to need a little tuck. *(Rings phone)*

GEORGE: Elliott, use your own phone.

ELLIOTT: I need it clear in case I get a call.

GEORGE: What if we get a call? *(George grunts, exits to yard)*

ELLIOTT: Busy! Damn! *(Hangs up phone, crosses to Helene)* Hey, Mom, those pictures you took at the beach. Outstanding.

HELENE: Thank you, dear.

ELLIOTT: Sure caught some great-looking women.

HELENE: Yes. I'm sorry I didn't have your card to pass out.

(Elliott can't be insulted, laughs. Exits to yard)

HELENE: George, help me with this. *(George comes back in. Together they will work on party)*

GEORGE: The boys seem to like Janie a lot.

HELENE: Yes.

GEORGE: She seems to like them too. I see she gives them equal time.

HELENE: I think Elliott gets a little more. I'm referring to time.

GEORGE: I'm not.

HELENE: *(Annoyed)* Can we talk about it later? We've got a dozen people showing up tonight and there's still a long way to go.

GEORGE: What are we supposed to do?

HELENE: About what?

GEORGE: Janie!

(It gets increasingly testy between them)

HELENE: I don't know! We've never had her type of live-in service before!

GEORGE: You better talk to her. It doesn't look good her wandering from one bedroom to the other.

HELENE: All right! I'll suggest she pick one and stick to it!

GEORGE: Oh, Helene, please! As long as she's here we incur some responsibility!

(Elliott has come in from patio, listens unnoticed to the argument)

HELENE: Then you talk to her!

GEORGE: I would, but I'm the wrong sex.

HELENE: Then talk to your sons!

GEORGE: It shouldn't be hard. Just be straightforward!

HELENE: All right, I'll try!

GEORGE: And for God's sake get her to put some clothes on! Everything that's supposed to be on the inside is on the outside!

ELLIOTT: How long has this been going on?

(Now Helene and George become aware of Elliott)

GEORGE: What?

ELLIOTT: You two fighting like that?

GEORGE: We are *not* fighting! Your mother and I do not fight!

ELLIOTT: Well, that explains it at least.

GEORGE: What?

ELLIOTT: Why I'm having so much trouble with my marriage. You two sure set a lousy model.

GEORGE: Now just a minute . . .

ELLIOTT: Just kidding, Dad. Man, are you uptight!

GEORGE: Your mother and I are doing just fine! And we'd be doing even better if there was less congestion around here!

ELLIOTT: Yeah, I noticed that. I'll talk to Michael. Shouldn't be here, he's ancient.

(Phone rings, green light activated)

ELLIOTT: Mine!

(He races upstairs to answer phone. Janie, scantily dressed, comes out of Michael's room, starts down as)

GEORGE: Fantastic! Elliott doesn't think Michael belongs here! Michael doesn't think Elliott belongs here . . .

JANIE: *(Bubbly)* Hi!

GEORGE: *(A look at Janie, scantily clad)* I wonder if I do. *(He exits to patio. Will work on setting up for party)*

JANIE: Can I do something for you, Mrs. Butler?

HELENE: I'm setting up for buffet. You can help with the silverware, if you like.

JANIE: *(Very grateful)* Gee, thanks! Thank you, Mrs. Butler! I'll do a good job, you'll see!

HELENE: I'm sure you will. *(She gives Janie silverware box)* Keith says you're into Doomsday. Just what does that mean?

JANIE: You know, I study about wild food and how to purify sewer water. Things like that.

HELENE: Sounds interesting.

JANIE: Actually I'm very optimistic!

HELENE: About Doomsday?

JANIE: Ahuh!

HELENE: About it coming or not coming?

JANIE: Either way! I'm really excited about the ways mankind can survive in a ravished world! Of course, we'd have to give up certain luxuries . . . Prongs up or down? *(As Helene looks puzzled)* The forks?

HELENE: Oh, up will be fine. Spoons too. Let the knives fall as they may . . . Janie, I've been wanting to talk to you.

JANIE: *(Immediately assumes)* I did something wrong, didn't I? Just tell me, I'll correct it!

HELENE: No, it's not that.

JANIE: It's all right, honestly! Mom's always pointing out my screwups. It's good for me to know.

(It doesn't take Helene long to read Janie, and be sympathetic)

HELENE: No, Janie, you didn't do anything wrong. But Mr. Butler and I were wondering if you told your parents you were here.

JANIE: Oh, yes! I phoned Mom and Butch and told them everything! Butch is the man Mom's married to. He's my step-stepfather. He's a two step because I have a one step in between. *(As they do the table, Janie speaks ebulliently, seeing the bright side, as is her way)* Mom's been married three times! She won't just live with a man. She'd rather marry a man she didn't love than live with one she did. She has a lot of self-respect that way.

HELENE: Yes, some people are like that.

JANIE: Butch drives an eighteen-wheeler. He's a very nice person. The one step was Walter. He was a very nice person too. When he ran off, he left his two daughters with Mom so they could help her when they grew up.

HELENE: Yes, that was nice of him.

JANIE: My real father's name is Carl. He just upped and went to Alaska when I was little and married an Eskimo lady. So that's neat! If I ever go to Alaska, I'll have a stepmother up there.

HELENE: Yes, that does sound quite neat.

JANIE: I'm real lucky when you think of it. Besides a real mother and father, I've got a stepfather and two stepsisters, a step-stepfather and two stepbrothers. I've also got a half brother who's part Aleut.

HELENE: Certainly makes for a full family.

JANIE: Oh, sure, it's neat! Of course, I hardly ever see anybody. *(Quickly)* Oh, it's not their fault! I just don't seem to fit in with all those people, being the way I am.

HELENE: *(Gently)* And how are you, Janie?

JANIE: Oh, you know. So independent. Wanting my own way all the time. Spoiled.

(Helene's heart is going out to her)

HELENE: I don't think you're that way at all. It's been no trouble having you here.

JANIE: Maybe you just haven't noticed.

HELENE: No, dear, I assure you I would have. But there is one thing I'd like to mention.

JANIE: I screwed up, I knew it!

HELENE: You did *not* screw up. It's just that . . . well, with three men in the house I think it would be better if you wore a little more clothes.

JANIE: Of course! I should have thought of that myself! Oh, I'm so embarrassed!

HELENE: It's all right. Just . . .

JANIE: I certainly don't want Mr. Butler to get all horny over me!

HELENE: No, it's not like that . . .

JANIE: That'd be terrible! Just awful! That's what Mom said happened to Butch! Sometimes I think that's why she told me to leave!

HELENE: This isn't like Butch . . . !

JANIE: Oh, no, I know that! Mr. Butler'd never try to get me into his truck! He doesn't even have a truck!

HELENE: Janie . . .

JANIE: Oh, that Butch is a creep! Eesh! He wouldn't even listen when I tried to explain I was into celibacy!

HELENE: What?

JANIE: You know, that new thing that's going around.

HELENE: Oh, I guess I hadn't heard . . .

JANIE: It never even occurred to him a person could enjoy the opposite sex in a nonphysical way! *(Suddenly not so sure)* It's all right, isn't it?

HELENE: What?

JANIE: Celibacy! Some people say it's abnormal or something.

HELENE: No, no, it's fine if it's what you choose!

JANIE: Gee, thanks, Mrs. Butler! I value your opinion a lot.

HELENE: But I am a little puzzled. Why? It seems so unusual these days.

JANIE: You know, I did a lot of the other. I thought it was time for a change. Besides, sex is so boring. Bor-ing! Oh, you fake it a lot. "Wow! Hey, was that great! What a rush!" Things like that. You know how guys are. If your eyes aren't rolling up into your head they think *they're* useless.

HELENE: So I've heard. How are you doing with it?

JANIE: Great! What a fantastic high! You and Mr. Butler should try it sometimes!

HELENE: We have.

JANIE: You have!? You and Mr. Butler tried celibacy?

HELENE: *(Drily)* Yes, dear. At times it's a natural part of married life.

JANIE: Gee, I had no idea! Fantastic high, isn't it?

HELENE: Maybe we're not doing it right.

JANIE: You know, Mrs. Butler, Elliott wants to make it with me.

HELENE: I know and I don't think it's very good behavior on his part. I'm sure you told him how you feel.

JANIE: He doesn't take it seriously . . . He's screwed up, you know. No discrimination. No wonder Nancy wants to dump him.

HELENE: Janie, what do you do all that time up in their rooms?

JANIE: Talk. Michael's teaching me kung fu. I'm teaching him which flowers he can eat . . . He's screwed up, too, you know.

HELENE: That's George and me. We play no favorites.

JANIE: Telling him he's a genius all his life. Mom told me I was a dunce. You love your parents, I guess you want them to be right.

HELENE: Yes.

JANIE: Sure is a lot easier to be a dunce, though. *(Janie, of course, has hit an important note)*

HELENE: Janie, I'm not sure what Michael is anymore, but I do know what you are not: a dunce.

JANIE: Gee, thank you, Mrs. Butler! Thank you so much! Sure is interesting though. Two guys in the same family. One tries to solve all his problems with his brains, the other with his dick. Too bad they can't divvy things up a bit. *(About party set-up)* Gee, everything is going to look so nice.

(George comes in from patio)

GEORGE: Okay, all set out there. Want to take a look?

JANIE: *(Covering up)* Excuse me! *(She runs up and into her room, pulling her shorts down over her buns)*

GEORGE: That's a nice girl.

HELENE: That child is a mass of insecurity. No wonder. She's had a family life out of Charles Dickens.

GEORGE: Helene, what are you doing now? Adding one when we're trying to subtract two?

HELENE: No, but it does make you realize how fortunate our family's been . . . Incidentally, you don't have to worry about the bedroom traffic. Janie's into celibacy.

GEORGE: What?

HELENE: I know. Took me so long to learn how to handle all that casual sex, I hope I'm up to this new revolution.

(She exits. Elliott comes out of his room, goes into Michael's, takes out Michael's phone)

ELLIOTT: Hey, can I use your phone?

MICHAEL: *(Annoyed)* Use your own phone.

ELLIOTT: Can't. Got a call coming in.

MICHAEL: Then use the one downstairs.

ELLIOTT: Got a call coming in on that one too. *(Into phone)* Nancy! Christ, it's been impossible to reach you! Look, I've discussed our problem with my mother.

(Nancy hangs up on him. Janie comes out of her room with books. Helene reenters so both she and George hear the following)

ELLIOTT: Unreal! Man, she sure slams down a mean phone.

MICHAEL: Face it, Elliott, you've got a major weakness: You're an asshole. *(Enters his room)*

ELLIOTT: *(To Janie)* What's the matter with you?

JANIE: Oh, you're so dumb when it comes to women. It's not that she doesn't want her space invaded. It's that she doesn't want it invaded by someone who's trying to invade everybody else's space.

ELLIOTT: And what's that supposed to mean?

JANIE: You know what it means!

(Janie storms into her room, slams door. Elliott bangs on Janie's door. Michael pops out of his room. Through following series of door slams, Helene's whole body quivers)

MICHAEL: Incredible! I'm trying to get some important work done! Is there no sense of privacy in this place at all!? *(Storms downstairs)* Is there no respect for the other person in the slightest!? *(To his parents)* What did you two do raising Elliott? I've never seen anyone so self-involved!

(Michael storms out of house, slams door. Meanwhile, Janie comes out of her room carrying sweater with books, slams door, starts down. Elliott follows her)

ELLIOTT: Where're you going?

JANIE: Someplace.

ELLIOTT: I'll drive you.

JANIE: You will not!

ELLIOTT: Look, I'm only trying to be friendly.

JANIE: No, you're trying to fuck me.

ELLIOTT: Honest. I'm only . . .

JANIE: Kaka, kaka . . . *(Janie exits, slamming door. Elliott exits after her, slamming door)*

HELENE: God, my whole body feels like a tuning fork! No wonder I can't paint anything but jagged lines! . . . You know what we've got in our kids: a couple of recidivists! I know we survived their growing up, I wonder if we can survive their growing down! *(Her deep conflict and dilemma)* God help me, George, I love them, I appreciate family unity, but the chemistry has changed. I can't stand the noise and the rapid movement. I tried, but I feel like a shell-shocked trooper myself. *(Definitely)* You're going to have to do something. You're the man of the house: You look like a man, you dress like a man, you snore like a man.

(George gestures as if to speak)

HELENE: No excuses, please! I've seen all the conciliation I can take—

GEORGE: *(Interrupting)* Helene, I have done something. I talked to Howard Atkins.

HELENE: *(Puzzled)* Howard?

GEORGE: His real estate business gets him all over town. He's seen it everywhere: Kids coming back. So if you can't get them out of the nest, you get the nest out from under them! *(From out of the closet triumphantly George produces an* ATKINS REALTY FOR SALE *sign. Helene is not in favor of this idea at all)*

HELENE: No, George, that's not the help I'm looking for.

GEORGE: *(Selling her)* We get a nice *one*-bedroom condo at the beach. You get that outside studio we talked about . . .

HELENE: No, George . . .

GEORGE: That's what the Wallaces did! Ten days after the "For Sale" sign went up Wendy got married again! It's going on all over. Downward mobility! It's the only thing keeping the real estate market alive these days!

HELENE: I love this house.

GEORGE: I do too! But sooner or later we're going to have to leave it anyway.

HELENE: Later.

GEORGE: Look, you asked me to come up with something and I've done it! I have come up with a very creative idea!

HELENE: You have come up with a lousy idea.

GEORGE: It'd solve the problem just like that and not one word would have to be said!

HELENE: That's exactly what's wrong with it! It is ducking the issue!

GEORGE: *(Don't be cute here)* It is not ducking the issue, it is finessing around it!

HELENE: I've got a better idea. Hang the sign on Michael and Elliott.

GEORGE: Okay, but with either of them we'd have to offer rebates! *(Keep anger up as he puts sign away)* Okay, okay, I thought it would give you freedom to paint. That's what's holding you up, isn't it? . . . Or is it something else?

HELENE: *(A little alarm goes off)* What did you say?

GEORGE: *(Knows he's said too much)* Nothing. I didn't say anything.

HELENE: Yes, yes, you did.

GEORGE: *(Getting out of it)* Oh, I don't know what I said. *(Changing tone softer)* Look, hon, in a few hours some of our best friends are coming over expecting an oasis from the Great Out There. Let's just forget the young adults until tomorrow at least and wallow in old times and double stingers. *(Touching her)* And then after every-one's gone maybe we'll have some time to be together, you know . . .

HELENE: Oh, I don't know, I just haven't been in the mood, I guess . . .

GEORGE: Oh, I know, I understand, I'm not . . . *(An idea)* Let's go to a motel! Pack an overnight bag, toss in a toothbrush, just like we used to before we got married!

HELENE: George, that was different. We had no place to go.

GEORGE: Honey, I'm not sure it's so different at all.

ELLIOTT: *(Offstage)* I just think . . .

(Janie and Elliott come flying back in)

JANIE: I don't care what you think about the idea! I'm not interested!

ELLIOTT: It's a dumb idea, that's all.

JANIE: Oh, how would you know!

(Michael comes bounding in)

MICHAEL: I've got it!

GEORGE: What?

MICHAEL: The problem.

HELENE: You've solved the problem nobody else could solve?

MICHAEL: No. But I can show it can't be solved.

ELLIOTT: What kind of a solution is that?

MICHAEL: It's new.

HELENE: But Professor Neumann said at the beginning it couldn't be solved.

MICHAEL: No. He said it *hadn't* been solved which isn't the same as it *couldn't* be solved. I can show it *can't* be solved which explains why it *hasn't* been solved showing moreover why it *won't* be solved. *(Excitedly explaining the math of the problem)* You see, I can show the problem is equivalent to the continuum hypothesis. It rests on the fact the cardinality of the algebraic dual space is the smallest cardinal number strictly greater than aleph-naught.

GEORGE: Michael, this isn't MIT, it is only West Los Angeles. Nobody knows what you're talking about.

ELLIOTT: Yeah, don't give us any more grief.

MICHAEL: I'm gonna phone Professor Neumann. *(Michael exits to his room. Red phone light will come on)*

ELLIOTT: I've got a problem. Janie wants to move out. Can you believe it?

JANIE: Two girls I know want me to move in with them. It'll be cramped, but I've decided to do it.

ELLIOTT: Why? She's got a perfectly nice room here!

JANIE: Sure, Mrs. Butler, it's neat!

ELLIOTT: Okay!

JANIE: Except he's always sneaking in on me at night!

ELLIOTT: To talk!

JANIE: Bare-assed.

ELLIOTT: I'm worried about her, that's all.

JANIE: Why doesn't he worry about me with his pants on?
(To Elliott) I do not screw around, even if I was screwing
around, with married men!

ELLIOTT: I know that, and I respect that, but can't I show
concern . . .

*(He touches her; she gives him the elbow. Meanwhile Mi-
chael's phone light has gone off and he comes out of his
room. Slowly, revealing nothing, he comes down)*

HELENE: *(To Elliott)* Elliott! *(To Michael)* Well?

MICHAEL: *(Dumbfounded)* He says I'm still wrong.

HELENE: Oh, dear.

MICHAEL: He says the argument's brilliant, but it doesn't
apply.

HELENE: What else did he say?

MICHAEL: He said I can come back. He said if I want I can work on more unsolvable problems. He said since there'll always be a lot of unsolvable problems around I can have a long career.

HELENE: *(Gently)* Sounds as though he likes you, Michael.

GEORGE: Sounds as though he's got kids himself.

MICHAEL: Sounds pretty damn patronizing to me! Well, the hell with it! Who cares? I hate math! *(To George)* I only got into it because of you, Dad.

GEORGE: *(Stunned by this turn)* Me!?

MICHAEL: Yeah, it was all your idea.

GEORGE: Now just a minute! I said go to college, I never told you what to study . . .

MICHAEL: I don't want to talk about it, it's too depressing . . .

GEORGE: Well, I do!

MICHAEL: Dad, let it go, will you? It doesn't matter. I don't have to go back anyway. Brenda's coming here.

(Zing! Helene and George look at each other. Inwardly George is steaming)

GEORGE: Oh, she is, is she? And when?

MICHAEL: As soon as she can get her stuff together.

GEORGE: No, her shit! As soon as she gets her shit together! Well, what a shame! What a damn shame! It would have been *so* nice to have her and her shit as a house guest, but . . . *(George has crossed to closet, takes out the* FOR SALE *sign, and jabs it into the sofa)*

MICHAEL: *(Puzzled)* What's that for?

GEORGE: The house. It goes up in front!

MICHAEL: Why?

GEORGE: That's how it's done, son. You get a real estate agent. You put up a sign . . .

MICHAEL: You're selling this house?

GEORGE: It's the only one we can sell without getting arrested.

MICHAEL: But why?

GEORGE: Your mother and I have our eyes on this cute little condo at the beach. Security building, sauna, rec room.

MICHAEL: *(Totally bewildered)* But where's Brenda going to stay? And Elliott and me and . . . ?

GEORGE: Guess you're just going to have to make plans.

MICHAEL: Wow, that's heavy.

ELLIOTT: Oh, hell, Dad, I think it's a great idea.

GEORGE: *(Surprised)* You do?

ELLIOTT: Sure. I've even got a buyer for you.

GEORGE: Who?

ELLIOTT: Me. Michael and me.

MICHAEL: *(Catching on to possibilities)* Yeah!

(Helene listens dumbfounded as her sons go on)

ELLIOTT: Sure! We'll take the old barn off your hands!
Give us some kind of sweetheart deal. It's all in the
family . . .

MICHAEL: *(Enthusiastically)* All right!

*(The brothers give each other the high five. Are caught up
in their plans)*

ELLIOTT: You and Brenda take over the master suite!

MICHAEL: We knock out the wall upstairs, make a suite for
Janie and you . . .

ELLIOTT: We'll share the dressing room out there. I can
run the mail-order business out of it!

MICHAEL: All right!

ELLIOTT: But don't worry, Mom, we'll clean out the
maid's room and any time you and Dad want to come
and visit, it's yours!

MICHAEL: Sure! Stay as long as you like. We'd love having
you around!

HELENE: They're not yo-yos! They're locusts! That's it! That's the absolute last straw! Sell them the house!? *(She picks up* FOR SALE *sign; to George, in abject frustration)* What's the matter with you!? Didn't you hear a word I said!? *(She begins to whack at him with sign. He flees, she pursues him)* I said I didn't want to sell the house! *(She whacks at him)* I said I was not going to be rooted out!

(The boys are alarmed. Janie watches open-mouthed)

MICHAEL/ELLIOTT: Mom!

GEORGE: *(Fleeing, but still mollifying)* It's all right! She's just having a fit!

HELENE: You bet your ass I'm having a fit! *(Whacking at the fleeing George: beginning to cry)* I will not live with them anymore! I can't stand half the things they do! *(Stops whacking at George: This is to him, not the Sons)* Elliott can chase all the girls he wants. I just don't want to see it! And Michael! Thirty years old, running back home to Mommy and Daddy, laying out his "suffering" like so much Tupperware! I can't take it! I can't watch them tripping all over their problems! I can't serve as emotional control center any longer, the mother machine is all worn out! . . . George, I'm telling you once and for all: Either they go or I do, make up your mind! . . . Oh, I think I'm going to bawl!

(Which she had been doing. She throws down the sign, grabs up her purse, and bolts. Everyone looks after her, stunned)

JANIE: *(At length; in awe)* Wow! Being a mother sure is terrific!

LIGHTS OUT

Scene 2

The same. A few hours later. Helene has not returned. A worried George is on the phone. Janie listens.

GEORGE: *(On phone)* Yes, yes. *(Though he is)* No, no, I'm not really worried. It's just that it's been a few hours and . . . Yes, I'm sure you're right, but you will let me know if you hear anything . . . Of course, Martha, I'll do the same. *(Hangs up)*

JANIE: What about Mrs. Butler's other friends?

GEORGE: I can see her going to Martha. I'm not sure about the others.

(Michael and Elliott come in from outside)

MICHAEL: Nothing. We cruised the whole neighborhood. We even went by the gallery.

JANIE: Did you check the bars?

ELLIOTT: Janie, Mom doesn't go to bars by herself.

JANIE: She may be starting now.

ELLIOTT: *(Dismissing her point)* Okay . . .

JANIE: What about the bus depots? That's where they looked for me when I ran away from home.

GEORGE: She did not run away from home. She was upset. She wanted to be by herself.

JANIE: I don't think they were trying to find me though. Just making sure I didn't miss the express.

MICHAEL: Dad, I'm sorry. I didn't mean to make it rough on you.

ELLIOTT: Yeah, me too.

GEORGE: Well, I'm sure Mom didn't mean everything she said.

JANIE: Sounded to me like she did!

GEORGE: All right, Janie.

JANIE: We get out of here or else!

GEORGE: There is not going to be "or else." Mrs. Butler is not going away . . .

JANIE: Then I don't think we should sit around doing nothing.

ELLIOTT: What should we do?

JANIE: Pack.

MICHAEL: Dad, do you want Elliott and me to cruise some more?

ELLIOTT: Yeah, we can keep looking.

JANIE: At times like this people usually go to lovers. If Mrs. Butler has a lover I'll bet that's where she is.

ELLIOTT: She hasn't got a lover.

JANIE: How do you know?

ELLIOTT: I know, that's all.

JANIE: God, sons are dumb. You can have a lover, Michael can have a lover, Mr. Butler can have a lover . . .

GEORGE: I haven't got a lover.

JANIE: Well, if she is with a lover, it's going to be a few hours yet.

GEORGE: Janie, please.

MICHAEL: I think she went to Dodger Stadium to see the ball game.

GEORGE: (Forbearance) Michael, there're a lot of places she might be. I don't think Dodger Stadium is one of them.

MICHAEL: Why not? She likes baseball.

ELLIOTT: (An idea) A movie! That's the perfect place! Sit in the dark and cry all she wants to!

MICHAEL: What's playing?

ELLIOTT: *(Annoyed)* What's the difference what's playing, Professor?

MICHAEL: Because you can tell by what's playing, moron, if it's a movie Mom might go to.

GEORGE: Look, this is no good. She's frustrated, she's angry, she's got a perfect right to go out and stay out if she wants to. I just wish she'd phone, that's all, and let us know she's okay . . .

JANIE: *(Simply)* Maybe she left the city.

(Everybody looks at her)

Maybe she went to the airport. A lot of people do that. Get on the first plane for wherever and go there. Change their identity, start a new life, and nobody ever hears from them again.

ELLIOTT: I like your other idea better.

MICHAEL: Yeah, let's go pack. *(He and Elliott head upstairs)*

JANIE: *(Cheering everyone on)* Sure! Line up our things by the door! When she comes back she'll see the suitcases and be happy!

GEORGE: I really don't think Mrs. Butler means for you to leave on a second's notice. This is not Simon Legree and Little Eva.

JANIE: Oh, that's all right, Mr. Butler. I'm used to making quick moves. *(Janie crosses to where George sits. She massages his neck muscles, working out the tension)* Now don't you worry about her. She's going to be fine no matter how it seems.

GEORGE: I am not worried about her and it doesn't seem like anything . . .

(Janie has placed her palm on George's head. Now she smacks her hand, jolting George a bit)

JANIE: Gee, if we go and Mrs. Butler doesn't come back, you're sure going to be lonely.

GEORGE: I am *not* going to be lonely! Mrs. Butler *is* coming back as soon as she feels like it! We are coming into a very satisfactory period in our lives . . .

(There is a sound outside the front door)

JANIE: She's here! She's coming back! *(Janie is activated, stages the following in heavy whispers)* Elliott, bring down some suitcases!

ELLIOTT: *(Upstairs)* They're still empty!

JANIE: It doesn't matter! It's symbolic! Line them up by the door! *(To Michael)* Run outside! Cut some flowers!

MICHAEL: There's no time!

JANIE: *(To George, admonishing him)* You should have a nice present for her!

GEORGE: How am I going to get a present now?

JANIE: Elliott, she's here! Hurry up!

(Having come down with empty suitcases, Elliott places them by front door)

JANIE: Now, everybody, line up! Smile! Everybody smile like we're so glad to see her!

(Everybody lines up, smiles big. The door opens. In comes —not Helene Butler—but Keith Butler, number three son. He grins broadly, holds a duffel bag, and a box of candy for his mother, wears the red woolen scarf Helene had given him before he left. Everyone is stunned)

KEITH: *(Brightly)* Hi!

MICHAEL: Keith!

KEITH: Michael! Elliott! What're you guys doing here?

GEORGE: What're *you* doing here?

KEITH: I ran out of chicken sandwiches.

JANIE: *(The only one who isn't family)* Hi. Keith, you can't stay. *(Starts shoving Keith out of house)*

KEITH: What?

JANIE: You can't, that's all, I'm telling you.

(Michael and Elliott help shove Keith out. Needless to say, Keith is thoroughly bewildered)

MICHAEL/ELLIOTT: No, you can't stay . . . Keith, you've got to get out of here . . . Don't even put your stuff down . . .

(Keith hits Elliott on head with candy box, breaks away)

KEITH: What are you talking about!?

GEORGE: Son, it's hard to explain right now, but . . .

KEITH: Where's Mom? What's the matter? What happened?

GEORGE: Nothing happened! She's all right!

JANIE: She just disappeared, that's all! But there's no reason to suspect the worst!

GEORGE: Janie, please, stop making things better!

MICHAEL: *(To Keith)* You can't stay, that's all!

JANIE: *(Indicating suitcases)* See! We're all leaving!

ELLIOTT: Yeah, you've got to let up on her, man! She's a person too. Hasn't she done enough already!? Isn't it time she lived her own life, for Christ's sake!?

KEITH: *(Totally confused)* What the hell are you talking about!?

MICHAEL: We're telling you you can't stay!

KEITH: I'm not staying! I only came back because I got a toothache!

GEORGE: What?

KEITH: I want to see the dentist.

GEORGE: *(This is a little much for him)* You got a tooth-ache in San Francisco and drove five hundred miles to see a dentist in L.A.?

KEITH: Yeah.

GEORGE: There must be two thousand dentists up there! Why didn't you see one of them?

KEITH: I don't know any of them.

GEORGE: And that's how you're grown up and handle your problems?

KEITH: Sure, Dad, but I don't drill my own teeth . . . Where's Mom?

JANIE: *(Glowing)* She's not here! She ran away! She made this totally bitching speech like the French Revolution and raised the sign . . .

GEORGE: Janie! Please! *(Janie scoots away to Keith)* We've got a little problem. We're working it out. There's nothing to worry about . . .

(Helene enters with pastry boxes. She will not see Keith who is behind her. She puts boxes on table)

KEITH: Hi, Mom.

(Helene goes rigid, then turns and sees another returnee)

HELENE: Hello, dear. This is a surprise.

KEITH: For me too.

(Keith gives Helene candy box. She thanks him. All crowd around Helene. Ad libs: "How are you? . . . Are you all right? . . . Sit down, rest")

HELENE: I'm all right. I'm fine.

GEORGE: Are you sure?

HELENE: Positive. First, I want to apologize . . .

GEORGE: Look, hon, that's not necessary . . .

HELENE: Not for what I said. I still mean every word of it. For the way I said it.

MICHAEL: I'm glad you did, Mom. I didn't even notice I wasn't wanted.

JANIE: Where have you been, Mrs. Butler?

HELENE: Marcel's.

GEORGE: *(Baffled)* You stood here pouring your soul out, practically knocked my head in with that sign, then went out to the pastry shop??

HELENE: *(Simply)* I need dessert for the party.

KEITH: What's been going on around here? I must have missed a hell of a lot being away.

GEORGE: *(Drily)* He came back because he got a tooth-ache.

HELENE: Oh. Which tooth, dear?

KEITH: I don't remember. The pain's stopped.

GEORGE: Maybe if you drive back to San Francisco it'll start again.

KEITH: Mom, I hope you don't mind, but I won't be hanging around. As long as I'm down here I'll go stay with Carol.

JANIE: We're going too, Mrs. Butler. We talked it over. We'll help you clean up after the party, then split.

ELLIOTT: Right! Come on, guys, let's get our shit together.	KEITH: *(To Janie)* What's been going on?
MICHAEL: Yeah, OK.	JANIE: Tell you later.

(The young adults start upstairs. Helene and George look on, all but in disbelief at what is happening)

JANIE: At least I've got a place to go. *(Exits to her room with Keith)*

ELLIOTT: Where you gonna go, Mike?

MICHAEL: I don't know. I'll have to figure it out.

ELLIOTT: Want to share a place with me?

MICHAEL: Are you serious? I can't stand your behavior any more than Mom can.

(The kids, having slammed their doors, are in their rooms. George and Helene, on their feet, look at each other. Is it possible the kids are going?)

GEORGE: You did it, hon. They're packing! They're going!

HELENE: I'll believe it, George, when the doors stop slamming.

LIGHTS OUT

Scene 3

The same. Four days later. Night. Helene sits slumped in an overstuffed chair, glassy-eyed, holding a snifter with a daiquiri in it. No one else can be seen. Long pause as Helene's "catatonic" state registers. Then the front door opens, George enters.

GEORGE: Hi. *(Sees Helene)* Oh oh. *(Comes in)* No movement?

HELENE: Not on last survey.

GEORGE: Then what *are* they doing? They're supposed to be packing!

HELENE: They have been. For four days. You could clear out the Hearst Castle in less time.

GEORGE: They're stalling, Goddamn it, that's what they're doing, dragging it out.

HELENE: Daiquiris in the pitcher.

GEORGE: Thanks. *(He will pour himself a drink)*

HELENE: Remember on Penny Drive when the kids were small? All the mothers on the block had small kids too.

Come four o'clock when all the kids were napping, all the mommies got stinko on beer.

GEORGE: Why do you bring that up?

HELENE: I don't know. *(Sips)*

GEORGE: *(Studying her with concern)* You okay?

HELENE: Oh, sure. Just sitting here, longing for the peace and quiet of Dodger Stadium.

GEORGE: Where's Elliott?

HELENE: Out.

GEORGE: Where's Michael?

HELENE: *(Indicating upstairs)* In.

GEORGE: Where'd Elliott go? Tell me. *(Hopefully)* To buy a plane ticket?

HELENE: Who knows? He runs in, uses the phone, runs out, runs in, uses the phone, runs out, runs in, uses the phone, runs out . . .

(Little hiccup. A pause. George doesn't like the tone of this whole thing)

GEORGE: Did you get out of the house today?

HELENE: Oh, sure! I drove Michael to UCLA. The water pump on his car went out. Then I drove Elliott to pick up Michael's car when it was ready so Elliott could leave his for servicing. Which left Michael without a car so I gave him mine and went out and bought some roller skates. *(She holds up her glass)* Top this for me, will you, George?

GEORGE: *(Takes her glass to refill it)* Have you been sitting here all afternoon drinking these things?

HELENE: *(Holds up candy box)* Have a rum ball.

GEORGE: I guess you didn't paint today.

HELENE: Who said I didn't!?

GEORGE: You did! Great! Where's the canvas?

HELENE: Over there.

(He goes to the canvas eagerly, looks at it. His expression changes)

GEORGE: This?

HELENE: Yes.

GEORGE: There's nothing on it.

HELENE: Look closely.

GEORGE: *(Does so)* That dot?

(She crosses to painting, turns it over, putting the dot in different position)

HELENE: *(Proudly)* That's it.

GEORGE: Well, it's . . . it's . . . very nice.

HELENE: You like it?

GEORGE: Oh, sure. It's just that it's . . . well, all your other work's been representational.

HELENE: I was going to do two dots, but I lost concentration.

GEORGE: I see.

HELENE: I guess from now on I'm a one-dot painter.

GEORGE: Maybe tomorrow you can do more dots.

HELENE: Tomorrow, I think, is the PTA and the orthodontist.

GEORGE: Let's at least look at the progress we're making. Keith's gone.

HELENE: Sure, but he wasn't living here to begin with.

GEORGE: Janie's gone.

HELENE: I know. I miss her.

GEORGE: Okay, the others are going too. They agreed to it and that's it.

HELENE: George, that was days ago. I don't think they even remember the conversation. You know Michael. By the time he gets to the end of a sentence he's forgotten what he said at the beginning.

GEORGE: Then we'll remind them, that's all. *(Indicating upstairs)* What's he doing up there anyway?

HELENE: Who knows?

GEORGE: Did you call him?

HELENE: He doesn't answer.

GEORGE: Did you try the door?

HELENE: It's locked.

GEORGE: Honey, it can't be. There's no lock on that door.

HELENE: Then he nailed himself in.

GEORGE: How do you know he's up there?

HELENE: Inference. Every so often the toilet flushes.

(Michael comes out of his room, goes down hall to the bathroom. Meanwhile, George has been studying Helene)

GEORGE: What else, Helene?

HELENE: It's almost nine o'clock, George. That's what else.

GEORGE: Traffic was murder.

HELENE: Oh, traffic was murder yesterday. No, that was a late client's meeting. Traffic was murder the day before.

GEORGE: What's happening here?

HELENE: I think we're about to have a fight.

GEORGE: Not me.

HELENE: Oh, that's not fair. You've got to cooperate with something around here. When Keith first left for Seattle I heard you plainly. You had a lot of free time, you said . . .

GEORGE: I do.

HELENE: Then you're spending it someplace else.

GEORGE: I am not!

HELENE: George, you're not an insignificant person. If you'd been here, I'm sure I would have seen you.

GEORGE: I have been here!

HELENE: I thought you'd come home early some days at least and take them for pony rides. You only made seven o'clock one night this week. Really, you're going to have to get more convincing with your excuses! For instance: A) Two thugs held me up at gunpoint, locked me in the trunk of my car, took me hours to get free . . .

GEORGE: Okay, I get your point!

HELENE: *(Painfully)* B) The Truth: The phones don't stop, the kids don't stop, Helene's a wreck all the time, I don't want to go home . . .

GEORGE: I never said you were a wreck, I'd never say a thing like that . . .

HELENE: George, are you screwing around again?

GEORGE: No!

HELENE: This time I won't stand for it, not for a second.

GEORGE: I am not screwing around! I have not been near a woman in who knows how long, and I might add, that includes you!

HELENE: Well, you're part-timing it around here, that's for sure, just as you did when the kids were little. You've gone recidivist yourself.

GEORGE: You keep using that word! I don't even know what it means!

HELENE: Maybe we can survive *their* growing down, I wonder if we can survive *your* growing down!

GEORGE: Oh, this is ridiculous! I am not growing down!

HELENE: By the time the kids grow up a second time we'll be fighting with canes!

GEORGE: We are not fighting! They are not kids! They are young—

HELENE: No, George, they are kids and they'll stay kids as long as they're here!

GEORGE: Oh, this is insane! Accusing me of screwing around! Accusing me of not pulling my weight around here! Well, I resent the hell out of that . . . !

HELENE: *(Not backing down)* Resent it all you want to, but it's the truth! You were always very good at laying off the kid problems on me using work as an excuse! Oh, George, please, give me some credit! I can recognize excuses when I hear them!

GEORGE: *(That unleashes him)* Oh, sure! Sure you can!
Hell, you ought to! You've been making your share of
them for a long time!

*(Her eyes go to him. The following comes out of George's
depths)*

I've heard them! Year after year! Even after the kids
started to leave! You want to paint, but you're stifled,
you're smothered! Like it's some kind of family conspir-
acy directed at you! You want to paint, so paint! Pick up a
Goddamn brush and use it! Whoever gets an ideal situation? Plenty of women have gotten things done with
heavier stuff on them than you. They paint, they run
businesses, they go into professions! But they sure as hell
don't do it by flying into fits! They do it the only way it
can be done: by doing it!

HELENE: Damn you, George. I guess you've been holding
back on that a long time.

(George is immediately contrite)

GEORGE: Oh, honey, I don't mean to be mean. I love you
. . . I always have, ever since I first saw you in that pale
blue dress across the dance floor. But you've got to face
something yourself. The only one stopping you, Helene,
is you, nobody else.

HELENE: *(Painfully)* I know that, George, I have always
known it, even when I have tried my hardest to deny it.

*(Her admission affects him. He crosses to her sympatheti-
cally. Tearfully now, she goes on:)*

George, being a mother and a wife is serious business. It can be all consuming. "I can't do anything else. I've got kids to raise, a home and a husband to care for." You're so busy you don't need excuses for not doing anything else, and even if you're not, excuses are still available . . . But that's not the case when the kids grow up and there's time. Excuses don't hold anymore. *(Deep feeling. Her most poignant plea for understanding)* That's where I am now. Fresh out of excuses and scared to death. I'm down to the bottom line having to face the fact that despite my grand pronouncements, there may be nothing left in me but one dot . . .

(George embraces her and makes his pact with her)

GEORGE: No, honey, no, there's plenty left. Plenty. Now you take care of getting it out and I'll take care of the boys.

(Elliott comes in the front door and begins to go up the stairs)

GEORGE: Elliott, wait right there. I want to show you the fine points of a common human endeavor. It's called packing.

ELLIOTT: No point, Dad. My stuff's out already.

HELENE: When?

ELLIOTT: You missed it, Mom. You were working on the dot. It's okay, I'm out of here.

HELENE: Are you going back to Nancy?

ELLIOTT: No, that's not going to work, I've got to face it.
But I did talk to her and I apologized straight down the
line for being such a shithead.

HELENE: That was very nice of you.

ELLIOTT: *(The same lovable Elliott)* Yeah, I know. 'Bye,
Mom. *(Kisses Helene)* Thanks for everything.

HELENE: 'Bye, dear. Thank you for . . . for . . . well, I
do love you even though sometimes it's hard to explain
why.

ELLIOTT: *(That is no put-down to him)* Great, Mom.
You're so great . . . *(To George)* Isn't she great? Well,
'bye, Dad.

(George crosses to door, opens it)

GEORGE: 'Bye, son.

*(George and Elliott shake hands. Elliott exits and George
shuts the door. Michael appears. George and Helene look
at each other, know Michael's a harder case. Through following, when appropriate, Helene will support George,
urge him on by gestures and asides. George begins)*

GEORGE: Well, Elliott's gone.

MICHAEL: Yeah, I know.

GEORGE: So what're your plans now, son? Guess you'll be
moving right on too.

(Michael doesn't answer. Exits to garage)

HELENE: What's he doing?

GEORGE: *(Looking after Michael)* Rummaging through the garage.

HELENE: What for?

GEORGE: Honey, I don't know.

(Michael returns, carrying a Coleman stove)

What's that?

MICHAEL: My Coleman stove. For cooking. I'm taking it upstairs.

GEORGE: What for? You're not going to be here much longer.

(Michael is calm, reasonable, and very serious in his reasoning through the following. George is anything but calm)

MICHAEL: I've thought it over very carefully, Dad, and decided I'm not going.

GEORGE: Michael, that's not for you to decide. That's for us.

MICHAEL: Dad, I don't think you should get high-handed about this. If you want to discuss it we should do so calmly.

GEORGE: I'm very calm, Michael . . .

MICHAEL: It's not as though we're a family who doesn't love each other . . .

GEORGE: Of course we love each other! But the decision of whether you stay or not is up to Mother and me.

(Helene indicates to George he's doing good . . . Michael is remarkably unperturbed)

MICHAEL: You know, that's very interesting. That's what I thought at first. I even packed all my things. Until I worked it through and realized I had as much right to be here as you. In fact, more.

GEORGE: Yeah? And how did you get to that?

(Michael is eager to explain his reasoning)

MICHAEL: Well, look. We moved here when I was 5. We've been here twenty-five years. That means I've been here eighty percent of my life. You've been here forty-five percent of yours. Ergo, I have thirty-five percent more right to be here than you.

GEORGE: Michael, there's something wrong about that . . .

MICHAEL: Dad, please don't press it. You see, Mom's been here fifty percent of her life. So the one with the least amount of rights around here is you . . . If you like I'll work it out for you on my calculator.

GEORGE: *(Getting worked up on his own now)* No, thank you! My calculator looks at it entirely differently!

MICHAEL: Dad, you're raising your voice . . .

GEORGE: My calculator's all about who pays the bills!

MICHAEL: Yes, I thought you might raise that point. I did some work on that too. You have a monetary outlay in bringing me up. A substantial one, I acknowledge it. But that's balanced off by the joys I brought you. Naturally I couldn't put everything down, but here are a few items that accrue to my credit. The first time I said "Da Da." My first steps. In fact, all the cute things I did as a child. *(Turns notebook page)* Report cards with "A's." First prize in the Science Fair, Regional Winner of the Chess Championship. In summation, all those things that enabled you to swell your chest in pride and say, "That's my son." . . . Granted, it's not exact, but ergo you did get some bangs for your bucks.

HELENE: *(Aside)* Don't argue it on his terms. He'll kill you.

GEORGE: *(Aside to her)* That "ergo" alone does me in!

(Michael is caught up in the pleasure of point, counterpoint)

MICHAEL: Of course, you could argue you're the father, I'm the son. Therefore you carry certain preferential rights *a priori* . . . Then, however, I'd be forced to counter with the fact I had no say in my birth. You and Mom took that on by yourselves.

GEORGE: I'm so sorry for not checking with you ahead of time!

MICHAEL: Dad, please, now you're being facetious which only points out the weakness of your position.

GEORGE: Michael, do you know what you're doing? You're building an ironclad case for abortion!

MICHAEL: You could, however, riposte by claiming my whole argument is spurious.

GEORGE: Or how about just plain screwed up!?

MICHAEL: Yes, you'd have some weight there. I am screwed up. I acknowledge that. But then, of course, I'd be forced to point out that you and Mom were responsible. *(Pause)* Face it, Dad, at child rearing you two were klutzes. I say that without rancor, but you owe me for that too . . . Naturally, it's impossible to put monetary value on damage to psyche. But as we're a loving family I'm sure we can work out restitution without calling in outside arbitration. *(George and Helene are stunned)*

MICHAEL: *(Very conciliatory)* Oh, look, we don't have to settle it all right now. We'll have lots of time to talk. I'll be around.

(Michael starts upstairs with his stove. But by now George has had it, is on his own, needing help from no one)

GEORGE: Wait! Wait there just one minute! . . . Sit down, son.

(Michael does so. George sucks it in and goes)

Okay, okay, kid, let me give it to you straight! One loving father to a loving son! You're screwed up, all right. Hell, that's a given. So's Elliott, God knows. So's Janie. *And* Mom and me! Christ, who isn't? So what else is new? All that does is make you one of the pack! *(Pause)* Mother and I did the best we knew with you. And you know what we owe you: zilch! Whatever your package of problems is, it's yours, kiddo, even if we did give it to you! So you can go on blaming us and everything and everybody, but the bottom line is you are responsible for yourself! *(Pause)* Go back to MIT, don't go back, drive a cab, go Hare Krishna, but whatever you decide from now on this isn't your home base anymore! Now put that in your calculator and work it through!

HELENE: *(Worried by George's ferocity)* George . . .

GEORGE: No, that's it! I mean it! The most he's got here from now on is a pit stop! He can check in, change his oil, pump up his tires, then back out again onto the fast track! Ergo! A priori!

(Pause. Michael sits there frozen. It's hard to know what effect George's outburst has had on him. Even George and Helene don't know. Helene, "the mother," again looks at Michael closely)

HELENE: *(Worried)* Michael . . .

MICHAEL: *(Softly)* All my life I've loved math. I loved those hours with my books and my blackboard, working out problems that most people in the world can't even come close to understanding. I loved, you know, being special like that. I thought I could solve problems that had never been solved, that I could open new vistas, be an . . . Isaac Newton. *(He begins to tear)* They're real good back at MIT, Dad. They're better than I thought. I'm afraid. I'm afraid I'm not good enough, that I can't cut it. It's not that I don't want to be there, I do. Oh, hell, I can take the blizzards, it's not that. I'm afraid I don't really belong.

(Pause. Then George picks it up softly)

GEORGE: Michael, we've all been afraid at times. When I look at it, the biggest failures of my life came about because I was afraid. Maybe that's what growing up is: learning to be less afraid.

(Michael looks at his father, rises, and starts upstairs. Helene takes a step toward her son, but George stops her with a touch. Michael goes into his room, shuts the door)

HELENE: Oh, George, I feel horrible.

GEORGE: I know.

HELENE: What should we do? Go on up. Talk to him. Tell him he can stay until he works things out at least. *(She has slipped back)*

GEORGE: No.

HELENE: George, he's suffering. I can understand how he feels.

GEORGE: *(So is he, but he's firm)* I know he is, Helene, but no. This is right. He has to finish his growing up someplace else.

(The red light of Michael's phone has come on. George's and Helene's eyes go to it. They know he is making a phone call. The light stays on for a while, then goes off. George and Helene wait. Now Michael's bedroom door opens. He comes out, carrying his things, and starts down)

HELENE: *(On seeing Michael)* George . . .

(George stays her with a gesture, keeps her from going to Michael)

MICHAEL: *(Simply)* I phoned Professor Neumann. I explained why I left. I told him straight out I wasn't sure I could make it, but I wanted to come back and try again.

GEORGE: What did he say?

MICHAEL: He said he wasn't sure I could make it either, but I'd have a better chance if I worked on problems that could be solved.

(They laugh, tension broken)

HELENE: I was right. He does like you.

MICHAEL: Oh, I don't think it had anything to do with me specifically. He says they've learned to expect panic from the West Coast.

GEORGE: Sounds like a great guy, Michael. I hope someday I'll get to meet him.

MICHAEL: Well, if I hurry I can catch the Red Eye. 'Bye, Mom.

HELENE: 'Bye, Michael. *(She kisses him)*

MICHAEL: I can phone you, can't I?

HELENE: *(Misty-eyed)* You better.

MICHAEL: 'Bye, Dad.

GEORGE: 'Bye, son . . . Michael, I love you.   **P 23**

(Father and son embrace. Hold. Then Michael breaks and goes)

GEORGE: How do you feel?

HELENE: *(Tearfully)* Fine.

GEORGE: Me, too, but I'd feel better if I was sure he could find his way to the airport.

(She laughs. He turns to her. At last, alone together)

Now you and me, Helene. You will get to the Louvre in Paris, the Prado in Madrid.

HELENE: Will I, George?

GEORGE: And the Hermitage in Russia . . . and the Tate.

HELENE: Maybe kids aren't forever after all.

GEORGE: Maybe.

HELENE: *(The mother)* They are sweet though, aren't they?

GEORGE: *(The father)* Bittersweet.

HELENE: *(Touching him)* I'm so glad of one thing though: We didn't eat them when they were little.

(He laughs. She rises, looks at him, nudges him)

Well, come on, George, let's go fool around. *(She exits toward bedroom, as he smiles)*

CURTAIN COMES DOWN